Presented To:

_____

_____

By:

_____

_____

Date:

_____

_____

Lift Me Up

Printed in the United States of America

Second Printing: August 2019

Unless indicated, Scriptures taken from the Kings James Version

Lift Me Up

Me

Up

Lift Me Up is a short weekly read of 52
inspirational topics

By: Loretta Earl-Miller

The Introduction to "Lift Me Up"

In 2016, I was inspired to write a weekly blog on Facebook called Lift Me Up. My first writing posted on January 2, 2017. I wrote on subjects I felt were relevant and of interest to my readers. I didn't want them to necessarily agree with me but to at least give pause and thought to what I was trying to convey. I wanted them to feel that those few minutes reading my words on Mondays were not a waste of their time. I didn't want to convince anyone that I was totally correct on my perspective of scripture, but my prayer was that no matter your opinion or belief you would still be encouraged and lifted up after reading my words.

The fuel that inspired me to write 'Lift Me Up' each week was the feedback from my readers. My most pleasant surprise was the response received from pastors and their spouses. Knowing that so many in ministry were following my blog convinced me that just maybe my thoughts were not so far off. This is what inspired me to take these writings and place them in a book.

I have formatted the topics of my book differently than my blog. My first topic 'Good For Nothing' questions whether or not you will make it to heaven if you have never won a soul. Perhaps you feel that you have had no impact in the growth of the church. My prayer is that you will rethink those feelings after reading this blog. I was in high school when I was invited to church by Hope King. Many of my family and friends gave their lives to Christ as a result of this invitation. Never should we put a count on the impact of our witness by numbers. It is impossible to put a number on Hope's one witness.

I invite you to take this journey with me. After you explore the words God has placed in my heart my desire is that you will say, 'truly Loretta Earl-Miller has lifted me up!'

SPECIAL DEDICATION
"To My Family"

My first dedication is to one of the finest Christians I know. I made this statement about him to a dear friend. I said everyone should meet Fred Miller. He is one of the nicest guys you will ever meet. I didn't know twenty years ago that the Lord was preparing me for an unforeseen journey that would change my life forever. The first year that I was married to Fred, I complimented him for his love and genuine concern for me. I asked, where did you learn to treat a woman so kindly, he said, Loretta, my father LOVED my mother. During my writing of Lift Me Up, I would send him a copy of each week's message. He would always have something positive to say about my writing. I will be forever grateful to the Lord for bringing him into my life. Mr. Frederick Miller, I love you more than you'll ever know. And thank you for blessing me with my gorgeous bonus daughter, Rosette Miller. Rosette, I love you and pray for you always.

My second dedication goes to my two children, Doysha Chanel and Terran Nathaniel Earl. They didn't know they were the motivation that held me together when I was going through one of the most devastating trials of my life. I knew twenty years ago that my reaction to the transition that had taken place in our lives would have a negative or positive effect on them. During that time, I will never forget the Lord speaking to my heart and saying the best thing you can give your children is your continuous walk with me. I wanted them to know that no matter the hardships you may experience in this life, you can still hold your head up and continue to walk upright before the Lord with dignity. Thank you Doysha and Terran. I love you so much. And I would also like to thank you both for giving me five of the most beautiful grandchildren a grandmother could ever be blessed with. I love you Jared, Allyn, Nyana, Typhen and Zyah.

My third dedication is to Attorney Karrah Herring, my niece. Her input and editing gave life to my weekly blogs. However, I am sure that after fifty two weeks of editing she was thrilled when I told her that I would be ending my weekly blog at the end of the year. Thank you so much Karrah for your time and sacrifice.

My last dedication is to all of my friends and family who have prayed and interceded on my behalf over the years. If I named everyone, I would have to add four additional pages. I love you all.

A Special Note From the Author's Daughter:

Doysha Chanel

In life, peace is predicated on many things; environment, state of mind, and for many, a connection with a higher power. Peace helps to sustain economic development, ensures social order and creates a sense of security. The world however, has experienced many forms of distress, such as poverty, hunger, political turmoil and the most egregious of all, violence. Violence causes over 1.6 million deaths worldwide each year [Krug EG et al., eds. World report on violence and health. Geneva, World Health Organization, 2002. Via CDC]. This statistic alone creates a sense of upset and despair. In these tumultuous times, many have nowhere or anyone to turn to. Sometimes the idiosyncrasies of religion, the very thing meant to bring peace, create a barrier, and confusion sets in.

In Lift Me Up, Loretta Miller explores acceptance from the Holy Spirit and sheds light on key components to encourage the downtrodden, and heavy-laden. Over the years I have grown to appreciate her calling in life. As a child, I didn't realize the effect her ministry had, I just knew she traveled a great deal. Today, I see what the Holy Spirit gifted me was also a gift for the world.

A Special Note From the
Author's Son:

Terran Nathaniel Earl

The greatest thing I ever learned from my mother is love one to another. She has shown me this every second of my life by example. I do not know a human on this planet with a greater giving spirit or the ability to inspire and encourage unconditionally like my mother. Very few are born with a winning lottery ticket such as mine.

Many call my birth mother, mother, because of her faith, love, and leadership over the years. She continues to show an unwavering compassion for all people. In this book, I hope for whoever reads this, that you grasp at least a small portion of her love, that has uplifted so many people.

TABLE OF CONTENTS

Lift Me UP Week 1

Good For Nothing

Greetings ladies and gentlemen. Before you continue reading, take note of this disclaimer: The statement I am about to make is to bring out a point and not to be taken literally. Did you know the Bible says after you leave this life and you have not won a soul to the Lord that you are good for nothing? The Bible says in Matthew 5:13, "Ye are the salt of the earth; but if the salt have lost its savour, wherewith shall it be salted? It is thenceforth good for nothing, but to be cast out, and to be trodden under foot of men."

Someone may ask, why shouldn't I take this literally? Many years ago, I too took my previous statement quite literally. My thought process was, you witness to an individual at school they get saved, that's one soul. You witness to another person on your job and they get saved, that's two souls. That's how I counted my success in soul winning, but I don't believe the Lord counts that way. This session is to encourage those who cannot pinpoint an individual they have won to the Lord. Matthew 5:16 says, "Let your light so shine before men, that they may see your good works, and glorify your Father which is in heaven." If your light is truly shining before men, you really have no idea how many people you have won or helped lead to the Lord. Years ago, James Kilgore's (a small boy) father's car broke down while his family traveled and evangelized in the state of Idaho. The mechanic/owner of an auto shop was getting off work and told them he could not help them until the morning. The mechanic allowed James and his family to sleep in the car in his garage. He also told them not to steal any of his tools and that he would have to lock them inside the building. Much more happened, but this is the short version. And even though the mechanic was not very friendly toward James and his family that night, they maintained their Christian character. Many, many years later James Kilgore returned to Idaho as a grown man and Pastor, and told this story as he was ministering to an audience. After the message, a man came crying and fell on his shoulder and said, "Pastor Kilgore, I am the man that did not help you that night. I want you to know that I am now saved." The Kilgore family did not preach or teach that night, but it is evident to me that their light was shining.

As spirit-filled Christians, the Lord gives us power and commissions us to be witnesses. He also tells us to go out into the highways and hedges and compel them to come. Let us not count by numbers but by how bright our light is shining. Shine bright this week! Your light may be the very twinkle which leads someone to Christ.

_____

_____

_____

Lift Me Up Week 2

Mr. Speaker, The President of the United States

I believe this week's topic will not be as controversial as last week. However, I am certain to ruffle a few feathers.

America, America God shed His grace on thee! And crown thy good, with brotherhood from sea to shining sea! This message is for those of you who declared, along with 23 celebrities from Hollywood, if Donald Trump (who I did not personally vote for), becomes president of the United States, you were moving out of the country. Before you leave, let me try to stop you at the border. Please make sure the country you move to has freedom of religion, freedom of speech, freedom of the press, freedom to petition, etc. because regardless of the current state of our country, we are afforded those precious rights. And now for those who believe the Bible is the unadulterated word of God, take a deep breath (don't hold it too long) and start praying for President Donald Trump, as the word of the Lord directs us to do so. First Timothy 2:1-3 reads, "I exhort therefore, that, first of all, supplications, prayers, intercessions, and giving of thanks, be made for all men; 2.) For kings, and for (ALL) that are in authority; that we may lead a quiet and peaceable life in all godliness and honesty. 3.) For this is (GOOD) and (ACCEPTABLE) in the sight of God our Savior." It may not be good and acceptable in your sight, but it is definitely good and acceptable in God's sight. The scripture doesn't even tell us that we have to agree with our leaders. But as true Christians, we must intercede and pray for the leader of our great nation. You can turn on local and national news and see turmoil and unrest in our country. It is imperative now more than ever, regardless of your position on the political spectrum that we intercede for our president, our government, our local communities (spiritual and natural) and our families. America, America God shed His grace on thee! And crown thy good, with brotherhood from sea to shining sea! Let us pray!

_____
_____
_____
_____
_____
_____
_____
_____
_____
_____
_____
_____
_____
_____
_____
_____
_____
_____

Lift Me Up Week 3

Eternal Security, Are You Sure?

There is a question that has been asked of me many times since I have been saved. That question is, do you believe in eternal security. For those of you who may not be familiar with the terminology, you may recognize it by this saying, "Once saved always saved." I have had the opportunity to converse with two spirit filled Bishops and several friends on this subject. One Bishop was adamant that eternal security is biblical. The other felt believers of this teaching were in err. I feel ill equipped to give an opinion on the matter, and I do not write this week's passage to rally supporters of one Bishop over the other. However, I believe John 10:27-29 articulates a few of the foundational scriptures used to back up this belief of eternal security with Christ. It reads, "My sheep hear my voice, and I know them, and they follow me; and I give unto them eternal life; and they shall never perish, neither shall any man pluck them out of my hand. My Father, which gave them me, is greater than all; and no man is able to pluck them out of my Father's hand." I won't debate as to which Bishop is correct, nor will I attempt to resolve the matter with my personal opinions. Nevertheless, if you are seeking heavenly guidance on eternal security with Christ, I would encourage you to delve into God's word and read Revelations 2:20-21 which tells us that Jezebel was not lost because of her fornication, she was lost because she repented not. First

Timothy 5:24 says, "Some men's sins are open beforehand, going before to judgment; and some men they follow after." God has not called me to judge anyone's actions or their place in eternity. If we seek to understand God's opinion on the matter, the ONLY opinion that matters, let us search the scriptures; for in them ye think ye have eternal life.

_____
_____
_____
_____
_____
_____
_____
_____
_____
_____
_____
_____
_____
_____
_____
_____
_____
_____
_____
_____
_____
_____

Lift Me Up Week 4

Show Yourself Friendly

I'm sure many of you would agree when I say there is nothing more beautiful in this life than a genuine friend. I have been blessed with many during my lifetime. I asked myself this question, "What makes a good friend?" For me it is the trust I have in that individual.

Proverbs 18:24 says this regarding friends, "A man that hath friends must show himself friendly: and there is a friend that sticketh closer than a brother." Please note the reference to friend in this passage is plural. The author is highlighting that because of his friendliness he had more than one friend. It comforts me to know that through trying times I can call on my friends for compassion, love and support. A true friend does not have to know the gory details of your despair. Nor does a good friend have to talk to you every day of your life. But a good friend, regardless of the issue or the length of time that has passed since your last conversation, will immediately begin to intercede for you when they sense the need. For those who may say Jesus is the only friend I need, Jesus himself would disagree with you. He said this to His disciples in John 15:15, "Henceforth I call you not servants; for the servant knoweth not what his lord doeth: but I have called you friends." There was also a disciple described in John 13:23 whom Jesus loved. We know Jesus loved them all but there was something special about this particular disciple. It is also evident to me in scripture that Jesus was a close friend to Mary Magdalene.

You may ask why the emphasis on a need for friends. The answer to that question can be found in Ecclesiastes 4:9-10, "Two are better than one; because they have a good reward for their labour. For if they fall, the one will lift up his fellow: but woe to him that is alone when he falleth; for he hath not another to help him up." In the day and time we are living where the spirit of the age is pushing a divisive and separatist agenda, we desperately need the love, support and camaraderie of our fellow brothers and sisters. I honestly believe someone in your inner circle is praying for a friend. Could that person be you?

_____
_____
_____
_____
_____
_____
_____
_____
_____
_____
_____
_____
_____

Lift Me Up Week 5

Hurry Up Trial

Have you ever gone through a test or trial where you thought to yourself, "Lord when will I ever get through this?" Or maybe you are in a situation right now where you're singing the words of Smokie Norful's song, "Not a second or another minute, not an hour or another day, but at this moment with my arms outstretched, I need you to make a way, I Need You Now."

I have always heard trials and tribulations are for the testing of our faith. I suppose this is true to a certain degree. But if we are honest, we will admit that sometimes when we're going through, the only thing we are thinking about is quickly passing the test and finding victory on the other side. Amen!

If you're going through at this moment, let me say this first, "Don't give up!" Sometimes in a trial you feel as if you are going in circles. Israel had to feel this way while Moses was leading them in Deuteronomy 2:1-3. Moses is talking to them and saying, "We turned, and took our journey into the wilderness by the way of the Red Sea." He then says, "As the Lord spake unto me you have circled mount Seir many days." Can you imagine circling a mountain for many days and seeing the same thing each time? You see the same cliffs, the same stones, the same crevasses, and then turn the corner only to see them all over again! As frustrating as it had to be, Israel continued walking. Then God intervenes and tells Moses they have circled the mountain long enough. God is intervening in your trial to let you know you have been in this battle long enough, you have carried this burden long enough. This darkness has hovered over you long enough! In addition to overcoming the frustrating conundrum you're in, God wants to guide you to total victory. When you continue reading the passage you see God spoke a powerful word to Moses and the children of Israel. The word He speaks to them is TURN. Not only does He tell them to stop going in circles, but He instructs them on which way to turn. He doesn't tell them to go east, west or south, but He tells them to turn northward. Whenever you hear someone say go north, it also means "up." When you look up your eyes will be lifted unto the hills from which cometh your help, your help cometh from the Lord.

_____

_____

_____

_____

_____

_____

_____

_____

_____

_____

_____

_____

Lift Me Up Week 6

Worry Versus Prayer

Greetings Brothers and Sisters! In Sunday school we used to sing a very simple song that says, "Why worry when you can pray, trust Jesus He knows the way, don't be a doubting Thomas just stand upon His promise, why worry worry worry worry when we can pray." I believe this song would have been better suited for the adults to sing during the main service. Adults are the ones with bills, bad bosses, broken-hearts and so many other pressures. After all, most children in Sunday school are only worried about what they are going to eat after church and when they will be able to play. Philippians 4:6 says, "Be careful for nothing; but in everything by prayer and supplication with thanksgiving let your requests be made known unto God." The ISV interpretation of the Bible says, "Never worry about anything. Instead, in every situation let your petitions be made known to God through prayers and requests, with thanksgiving." Worrying is a waste of your life. Turn it over to God and watch His peace come in and sweep worry out.

I would like to end this week's Lift Me Up with ten "do not worry" quotes that I found to be quite inspirational. Feel free to share with your colleagues, family and or friends.

1. "Worry often gives a small thing a big shadow."

2. "Worry is like a rocking chair: it gives you something to do but never gets you anywhere."

3. "People become attached to their burdens sometimes more than the burdens are attached to them."

4. "Sorrow looks back. Worry looks around. Faith looks up."

5. "Rule number one is, don't sweat the small stuff. Rule number two is, it's all small stuff."

6. "A day of worry is more exhausting than a day of work."

7. "No amount of regretting can change the past, and no amount of worrying can change the future."

8. "Every tomorrow has two handles. We can take hold of it with the handle of anxiety or the handle of faith."

9. "Do not anticipate trouble, or worry about what may never happen."

10. "We would worry less if we praised more."

_____

_____

_____

_____

Lift Me Up Week 7

Mother's Day, But I'm Not A Mother

Greetings Brothers and Sisters! Mother's Day is just around the corner. For most of us this is an exciting and memorable day. But all do not share the joy that many of us experience on this day. There are those who will not attend church because they are not a mother. Others will not come because their mother is no longer with them. I love the way my sister commemorates Mother's Day at their church in South Bend, IN. They use it as a day to celebrate all women. And after reading about the founder of Mother's Day, she is correct in doing so. Some of you may already know this story, but I would like to share it with those who are not familiar with it. Anna Marie Jarvis was the founder of the Mother's Day holiday in the United States. Her premise for celebrating this day was her love and appreciation for her mother, Ann Jarvis. But to the surprise of many Anna Marie Jarvis was not a mother. Her mother was a Sunday school teacher, social activist and founder of the Mother's Day Work Clubs. As a woman defined by her faith, Anna's mother was very active within the Andrews Methodist Episcopal Church community. It was during one of her Sunday school lessons in 1876 that her daughter, Anna Jarvis, allegedly found her inspiration for Mother's Day. As Anna's mother closed her lesson with prayer, she prayed, "I hope that someone, sometime will found a memorial mother's day commemorating her for the matchless

13

service she renders to humanity in every field of life. She is entitled to it." These words stuck with Anna Marie for years, and in 1907 Anna began an aggressive campaign to establish Mother's Day in the U.S., ultimately proving to be successful. While she never had her own children, many referred to Anna as "The Mother of Mother's Day." Please take time to read additional information regarding the life of Anna Jarvis. It is a fascinating read.

Let me wrap up this week's session with words of appreciation to all individuals who have been instrumental in nurturing a child. This could be mothers, fathers, siblings or anyone who has encouraged, inspired or motivated our children. We all know that you don't have to birth a child to be a Godly mother. My brother was a wonderful father who nurtured his six children after he was faced with the responsibility of raising his children alone. While not a mother, he was able to stand in the gap of that missing figure. I am certain there are countless other stories of people who were raised and or mentored by aunts, neighbors, teachers, older siblings and the list goes on. You yourself may not have birthed a child, but act as a mother figure for many in your family, church or community.

I will leave you with this final thought. If you are blessed to be in the life of a child, remember to train them up in the way they should go: and when they are old, they will not depart from it. Proverbs 22:6.

Lift Me Up Week 8

Living Above Sin

I want to begin by saying this week's Lift Me Up session will no doubt be a little controversial. And I don't want anyone to misconstrue what I am going to say. However, I hope this will encourage the new Christian or even the seasoned saint who is struggling with their flesh. Let me pause here and highlight I emphatically believe Galatians 5:16 which reads, "This I say then, walk in the Spirit, and ye shall not fulfill the lust of the flesh." I have not always walked in the spirit, but I have sincerely tried to walk upright before the Lord. Let me also add, in all my years of being saved, I have not found a scripture to justify willful sin.

When the Lord saved me, I was taught we could live above sin. What an enormous pressure and unrealistic standard, especially for someone new to Christ. There is no way to describe the guilt I felt at seventeen years old when I fell as a new Christian. As I began to grow in the Lord, I began to study God's word for a deeper understanding of my walk with Christ. Not only did I begin to comprehend His word, I also found a new word I had heard very little about, GRACE. You can imagine the joy I felt when I read and understood the words in First John 2:1, "My little children, these things write I unto you, that ye sin not." There is no question in my mind that the Lord wants us to live a life free from sin. But John continues to write, "And if (not when)

15

any man sin, we have an advocate with the Father, Jesus Christ the righteous." To be human is to err and I believe as long as we are in this flesh we will all have to fall on our knees at the throne of GRACE. If you are an individual who believes you can live above sin, you would also have to believe there would NEVER be a reason for you to repent as a Christian. I encourage you to strive daily to live a Christ like life. If you find yourself falling from the grace of God, don't beat yourself up, but rather open your bible to First John 1:9 which says, "If we confess our sins, he is FAITHFUL and just to FORGIVE us our sins, and to cleanse us from all unrighteousness."

_____
_____
_____
_____
_____
_____
_____
_____
_____
_____
_____
_____
_____
_____
_____
_____
_____

Lift Me Up Week 9

Search Me Lord

Greeting Brothers and Sisters! I sat in the auditorium of a beautiful temple this week and was in awe of the structure and architecture of this building. I was only there a few minutes before I began to think about First Corinthians 3:15 which says, "Know ye not that ye are the temple of God, and that the Spirit of God dwelleth in you?" I realized the beauty of the structure I was admiring could not compare with the temple (my body) that the Lord resides in. I also felt a spirit of conviction and a desire to remove any and everything that was in my temple that did not please God. I was reminded of a song we used to sing in New Good Hope Missionary Baptist Church in Buchanan, Michigan when I was a teen that I still recite in prayer to this day. The song was called "Search Me Lord." It simply says, "Oh search me Lord. Come on and search me Lord. Shine the light from heaven on my soul. If you find anything that shouldn't be, take it out and strengthen me. Cause I wanna be right, I wanna be saved and I want to be whole."

The Apostle Paul was not making a statement, he was asking a question and that question was, "Do you know that you are God's temple and that God's Spirit dwells in you?" I believe he wants us to continually remind ourselves that our temple is a memorial unto the Lord. How blessed we are to have the creator of the universe dwelling in the very midst of our being. When you prepare your home for guests to visit, if you're a good host, you scrub, clean, disinfect, wash sheets and blankets and remove any junk from plain sight. If we go to those lengths to prepare our homes for mere mortals, how much more should we scrub, clean and disinfect our temples for the most high King. This week, let's do some intense cleaning and preparation through the reading of God's word and through prayer and worship so the creator of the universe can dwell in a holy and acceptable temple.

_____

_____

_____

_____

_____

_____

_____

_____

_____

_____

_____

_____

_____

_____

_____

_____

_____

_____

_____

Lift Me Up Week 10

Never Alone

In the seventeenth-century, English author John Donnen, pinned a sermon entitled, "No Man Is an Island." In this sermon he says, "No one is self-sufficient." I believe we would call that person in today's vocabulary a hermit, (a person who lives in seclusion from society).

It saddens me when I hear saints talk about being alone or lonely. I have heard single women and men talk about their longing for companionship and human connectivity. Generally their statement is, if only I were married. But, I have also heard married women and men speak of being lonely. This is a testament to the fact that feelings of loneliness can be experienced in singleness or even within a relationship. The Lord knew we would all experience loneliness at some point in our lives. I believe that is why He gave us assurance through His word on how to escape it. I have ministered for years on a sermon about someone leaving you, or even worse, forsaking you. This is my quote on the matter, "It is a terrible thing for someone to leave you but it is devastating for someone to forsake you." There are numerous passages where the Lord reassures Israel that He will not leave them. One particular chapter in Deuteronomy 31:8, He doesn't just tell them He will not leave them nor forsake them, but He also tells them I will go before you. Amen!

If you are experiencing a season of loneliness in your life (and believe me it is only a season), please read Hebrews 13:5 for He hath said, "I will NEVER leave thee, nor forsake thee." NEVER means at no time in the past or future; on no occasion; not ever. Find peace in God's promise that, whether there are hundreds of people around you, a spouse, family, and friends or even if you're all alone, He is always present to love and comfort you!

_____
_____
_____
_____
_____
_____
_____
_____
_____
_____
_____
_____
_____
_____
_____
_____
_____
_____
_____
_____
_____

Lift Me Up Week 11

Let's Laugh

Greeting Brothers and Sisters! Have you ever been around Christians who very seldom smile, display very little joy or just feel like we all should walk around in sackcloth and ashes? If you know anyone in this category please share this week's Lift Me Up with them. Hopefully, you will put a smile on their face. I will never forget what the late Pastor Josephine Joshua shared with me about a smile. She said God never gave you a smile for you, it was always for others. Please join me this week as I talk about smiles and laughter.

I absolutely love what I read on HELPGUIDE.ORG this week in reference to laughter:

Laughter is a powerful antidote to stress, pain, and conflict. Nothing works faster or more dependably to bring your mind and body back into balance than a good laugh. Humor lightens your burdens, inspires hopes, connects you to others, and keeps you grounded, focused, and alert. It also helps you to release anger and be more forgiving.

Proverbs 17:22: A merry heart doeth good like a medicine. Psalm 126:2: Then was our mouth filled with laughter. Israel felt this way because the Lord had done great things for them.

I am ending this week's Lift Me Up with a few cute jokes that I believe will put a smile on your face.

After starting a new diet, I altered my drive to work to avoid passing my favorite bakery. I accidentally drove by the bakery, and as I approached, there in the window were a host of chocolates, donuts and cheesecakes. I felt this was no accident, so I prayed... "Lord, it's up to You. If You want me to have any of those delicious goodies, create a parking place for me directly in front of the bakery." And sure enough, on the eighth time around the block there it was! God is so good!

The secret of a good sermon is to have a good beginning and a good ending: and to have the two as close together as possible.

What did Adam say on the day before Christmas? It's Christmas, Eve!

Remember the Bible says there is a time to laugh. Let's connect with family and friends this week and have a good laugh.

_____

_____

_____

_____

_____

_____

_____

_____

Lift Me Up Week 12

Have You Heard?

I have always been amazed with Proverbs the 6th chapter, verses 16-19. When reading these passages in Proverbs, I don't believe there is any confusion as to what the Lord hates. He hates a proud look, a lying tongue, hands that shed innocent blood, a heart that deviseth wicked imaginations, feet that be swift in running to mischief, a false witness that speaketh lies. But when the writer (I am assuming Solomon) writes of the seventh thing that God hates he makes it very clear that not only does God hate that this individual sows discord among the brethren, he adds that it is an abomination unto Him. The Lord is saying not only do I hate it, it disgusts me.

He who sows discord among a brother is a person who is spreading, scattering, and broadcasting something about your fellow brother (or sister) in Christ. The definition of discord is to cause strife and hostility. The Lord never says this person is innocent of the accusation. However, He is saying that He hates the fact that you are spreading, scattering and broadcasting it. By doing this, not only do we bring harm to our brother in Christ, we also cause strife and hostility among others. I do not write this in judgment as not one of us is without fault. And I am sure many of us may have been guilty of this at one time or another. However, my goal with Lift Me Up is to give words of encouragement. If you know that a brother or sister has done something out of character for a Christian, please take them aside and privately encourage them to lay aside whatever weight or sin they have committed. Your intercessory prayer and private words of encouragement and care may be the very salvation needed for that soul which has gone astray.

_____

_____

_____

_____

_____

_____

_____

_____

_____

_____

_____

_____

_____

_____

_____

_____

_____

_____

_____

_____

Lift Me Up Week 13

Will The True Saints Please Stand?

This week I want to focus on the laymen and laywomen who have committed and sacrificed themselves to the building of the kingdom of God. As a former pastor's wife and pastor, I don't believe there is anything more rewarding to a spiritual leader than to have members in the congregation who understand what it means to be completely committed to ministry. I love the first book of Philemon. The Apostle Paul starts out by saying, "Unto Philemon our beloved, and fellow labourer..." He then addresses Apphia, and Archippus, "our fellow soldier, and to the church in thy house." I am assuming these labourers are related to Philemon. He continues by saying, "Grace to you, and peace, from God our Father and the Lord Jesus Christ!" He praises them for what they are doing in ministry. In his praise of his fellow labourers and fellow soldiers, he first says, "I have heard of thy LOVE and FAITH, which thou hast toward the Lord Jesus." I am certain that the Apostle Paul is not totally surprised at their love and faith towards Jesus. But the second thing that he admonishes them for is their love and faith toward ALL SAINTS.

The Apostle Paul was acknowledging the individual who may not have been front and center or receiving all the public accolades, but the individual whose quiet support and dedication to the body of

Christ was at the foundation of the success of the kingdom of God. What's so beautiful about these individuals is they genuinely do not seek acknowledgement from man. Their loyalty is truly unto the Lord. And because of their amazing dedication and allegiance to the work of the ministry, I want to personally speak for the entire body of Christ by saying, "The Lord bless thee, and keep thee. The Lord make His face shine upon thee, and be gracious unto thee. The Lord lift up His countenance upon thee, and give thee peace. Your commitment is appreciated and the kingdom of God thrives because of your continued dedication and willingness to serve your leaders and God's church."

_____

_____

_____

_____

_____

_____

_____

_____

_____

_____

_____

_____

_____

_____

_____

_____

Lift Me Up Week 14

Off Limits

Greetings my brothers and sisters! My subject matter choice for this week is generally considered taboo in the spirit-filled setting. It is very disappointing to me that this topic is off limits because many individuals have dealt with this personally or experienced it through close friends or family at some point during their Christian walk. The subject is depression, a disorder marked especially by sadness, inactivity, difficulty in thinking and concentration, a significant increase or decrease in appetite and time spent sleeping, feelings of dejection and hopelessness. When the Lord saved me, no one was ever depressed. Well, no one ever confessed they were depressed. To admit that you were depressed meant there was a deficiency in your spirituality. We encouraged these individuals to increase their prayer life and hopefully after a while their depression would go away. I have counseled and prayed with family, friends and church members, and I can personally testify that it is not that simple. Prayer is a necessary and powerful tool to combat depression, but sometimes we must utilize additional tools so we can gain the mental strength needed to refuse to surrender to defeat.

In First Kings chapter 18, one of the boldest prophets of the Old Testament, Elijah, prays to God to bring fire down from heaven to consume the sacrifice, proving to the prophets of Baal that the God he served was the true and living God. Elijah prayed this prayer, "Hear me, O Lord, hear me, that this people may know that thou art the Lord God." The Lord heard and answered his prayer. This had to be one of the most exciting victories for Elijah. And then I read the next chapter. The Bible says Jezebel threatens to kill him. After hearing this report, Elijah sits down under a juniper tree, and he requested for himself that he might die, saying, "It is enough, now, O Lord, take away my life; for I am not better than my fathers." Elijah experienced great victory, and then in the very next chapter he slipped into a state of emotional despair.

Elijah was not alone in his experience of emotional turmoil. Job, Jonah and Jeremiah also echoed words of death when they went through the lowest time in their lives. But all, including Elijah, received victory at the end of their journey. Why? Because they did not surrender to defeat.

If you have suffered with depression for a significant time in your life and have prayed and counseled with your pastor or spiritual leader, and you find yourself still battling a spirit of despondency, first know that you do NOT necessarily have a spiritual deficiency. Second, I encourage you to seek a Godly Christian counselor who can use their expertise, in conjunction with your prayers, to support and guide you to victory. Psalms 34:17 says, "The righteous cry, and the Lord heareth, and delivereth them out of all their troubles." God is listening. Utilize the spiritual and natural tools available to you so you can gain the strength to stand boldly and refuse to surrender to defeat!

_____

_____

_____

_____

_____

_____

_____

_____

_____

_____

_____

_____

_____

_____

_____

_____

_____

_____

_____

_____

_____

Lift Me Up Week 15

To Be Born or Not to Be Born

Many of you may be familiar with the pro-life march, "March For Life" which took place in Washington on January 27, 2017. How admirable it is for men, women and children to march for the sanctity of life. I pray that we all will petition the Lord for the lives of these innocent unborn babies.

My desire is to share with you why I believe some women find it easy to have not just one, but in some cases many abortions with little or no remorse. These women are generally pro-choice and in favor of the availability of a medically induced abortion as a means of ending a pregnancy. Many are comfortable with this act because doctors who perform abortions will say the fifth week of pregnancy, or the third week after conception, marks the beginning of the life of the baby.

Now for the disclaimer. As you know, I am not a doctor nor am I a scientist, and I definitely would not want anyone viewing my high school biology grades. However, I do believe I know a little something about the word of God. When you read Leviticus 17:14, you will see those doctors' theory totally goes against the word of God. Moses writes, "Ye shall eat the blood of no manner of flesh." I am certain the children of Israel wanted to know why they could not eat the blood of flesh. Moses makes this point very clear by saying, "For the (LIFE) of (all flesh) is the blood thereof." In other words, the life of every creature is in its blood, and without blood the fetus cannot begin to grow. I believe this scripture demonstrates the life of a fetus begins far before the third or fifth week as some professionals say, but at the moment of conception. Furthermore, Jeremiah 1:5 reads, "Before I formed thee in the belly, I knew thee; and before thou camest forth out of the womb I sanctified thee, and I ordained thee a prophet unto the nations."

Now, for those who believe there is no forgiveness for women who made the decision to have their pregnancy terminated, please read, Mark 3:28-29. There is only one unpardonable sin, and abortion is not it. God loves us dearly and His mercies are renewed daily. Our lives and the lives of those unborn babies are in God's hands. Let us not only march for life, but pray for life.

Lift Me Up Week 16

Relax and Meditate

Greetings brothers and sisters! This week I would like to touch on a subject that is interesting to me, but yet I do very little of. The topic is meditation. In prayer last week, I found myself praying about an issue which I needed specific clarity on. As I was talking to the Lord, I felt in my spirit that the Lord was directing me to be silent. I stopped praying and began to meditate on the situation. I went online to read what others had to say about meditation and ran into this story from Christian Today. "Overstressed Americans are increasingly turning to various forms of Eastern meditation, particularly yoga, in search of relaxation and spirituality. Underlying these meditative practices, however, is a worldview in conflict with biblical spirituality— though many Christians are (unwisely) practicing yoga". Please feel free to read the entire article online. It is in their 2004 November issue.

To meditate is to think deeply or focus one's mind for a period of time, in silence or with the aid of chanting, for religious or spiritual purposes or as a method of relaxation. Now let me share with you what the Bible has to say about meditation. One of the most quoted scriptures on meditation is found in Psalms 1:1-2 which says, "Blessed is the man that walketh not in the counsel of the ungodly, nor standeth in the way of sinners, nor sitteth in the seat of the scornful. 2 But his delight is in the law of the

Lord; and in his law doth he meditate day and night." The psalmist makes it very clear that if we're going to meditate, our meditation should be on His word. However, I do believe there are times during our personal devotion that we should sit and meditate on whatever it is that we are requesting from the Lord. Romans 8:26 reads, "Likewise the Spirit also helpeth our infirmities: for we know not what we should pray for as we ought: but the Spirit itself maketh intercession for us with groanings which cannot be uttered." I thought this was an interesting translation from the NLT which reads, "And the Holy Spirit helps us in our weakness. For example, we don't know what God wants us to pray for. But the Holy Spirit prays for us with groanings that cannot be expressed in words."

There are times during our daily devotion that we should be still and allow the Lord to talk to us. Because sometimes, our most still and quiet times are when God reveals His biggest plans and guidance for our lives. Psalms 46:10 says it best, "Be still, and know that I am God." If you want to read more about what God's word says about meditation, read Joshua 1:8.

_____

_____

_____

_____

_____

_____

Lift Me Up Week 17

Never Stop Praying

Greetings Brothers and Sisters! My subject this week is on prayer. Let me first say you will never be able to achieve a victorious Christian life over your flesh without a personal time of devotion. I have heard many in ministry give the minutes or hours that are required of a Christian to pray. I personally believe in quality over quantity. I believe it is the genuine intimate communion of your prayer that creates a solid channel of communication with God. While pastoring in Indianapolis, I did not put a time frame on how long our members should pray, but I certainly encouraged them to pray. However, I do know as you pray, you will find yourself praying longer and drawing closer to the Lord. I heard a pastor say years ago that you were not called to ministry if you could not pray for at least one hour a day. I believe the one hour of prayer was given to ministers because of the disciples in Matthew 26:40 where Jesus asked (Peter), "What, could ye not (watch) with me one hour?" Even though he ask Peter could he not watch for one hour, he was also encouraging them in the next verse to not just watch but watch and pray that they enter not into temptation. This passage lets me know that if we are sincerely praying consistently to the Lord, we will have power over our flesh.

I'm sure many of you have heard individuals say, don't get up from praying until you feel the presence of the Lord. If I took this statement literally, there would be times when I would never get up. My desire is to always feel God's presence when I pray. And there are times when we pray and we wonder if God is listening or if He's there. David said in Psalms 13:1, "How long wilt thou forget me, O Lord? Forever? How long wilt thou hide thy face from me?" If you ever find yourself in this state, remember it is only a trick of the enemy to make you feel as if God's presence is not there. I want to reassure you that God's presence is there. For you will find that same psalmist in Psalm 139:8-10 saying, "If I ascend up into heaven, thou art there: if I make my bed in hell, behold, thou art there. If I take the wings of the morning, and dwell in the uttermost parts of the sea; even there shall thy hand lead me, and thy right hand shall hold me."

If you don't feel a jerk or an unction of the Holy Spirit while you are praying, remember that this is a walk by faith, not a walk by feelings.

_____
_____
_____
_____
_____
_____
_____
_____
_____

Lift Me Up Week 18

Ouch! That Hurts

Greetings Brothers and Sisters! We all know the impact of words. Especially words that carry a negative connotation. I'm sure many of you will agree with me when I say that this highly quoted phase is in err: Sticks and stones may break my bones, but words will never break me. Coming up as a child, I heard it quoted as, "Sticks and stones may break your bones but words will never hurt you." No doubt a majority of us have been hurt by someone's sharp words in our lifetime.

I thought this was an interesting study on the effect of words that hurt. I want to first say I am absolutely terrified of needles so I was not surprised to read this in the WebMD report, "Words Really Do Hurt" April 2, 2010. -- "Sticks and stones may break your bones, but words *can* hurt you too," according to new research. A new study suggests merely saying, 'This may hurt a bit,' before receiving a shot may be enough to trigger a pain response in the brain long before any actual pain is felt." True or not, I agree with this wholeheartedly because tears swell up in my eyes before I even see the needle. Smile.

I believe that negative words can hurt you psychologically and even impact your physical health. We should be careful and cautious of the words we use to communicate. Ephesians 4:29 in the NIV gives us a very clear description on how we should talk to others, "Do not let any unwholesome talk come out of your mouths, but only what is helpful for building others up according to their needs, that it may benefit those who listen." This week, let us use the power of our words to build, encourage and show the love of God to our families, friends, co-workers and neighbors. Your kind words may be the healing needed to begin to reverse the effects of years of negative speech piercing their soul like sticks and stones.

_____
_____
_____
_____
_____
_____
_____
_____
_____
_____
_____
_____
_____
_____
_____
_____
_____
_____

Lift Me Up Week 19

God's Marriage to the Backslider

Greetings Brothers and Sisters! This week I would like to focus on a scripture that encourages us to never give up on the backslider. God does not give up on them and neither should we. The passage is found in (NLT) Jeremiah 3:14 "Return home, you wayward children," says the LORD, "for I am your master (The KJV says, "for I am married to you"), I will bring you back to the land of Israel--one from this town and two from that family--from wherever you are scattered." The Lord is telling Israel that even in their backslidden state 'I am still your husband.' This is truly an example of God's immeasurable love.

I had an experience last week in Boise, Idaho, that enlightened my thinking of a backslider. I listened to the heartbeat of a young man who has been away from the Lord. He shared with me how the Lord has been dealing with him. His personal testimony made me understand how the Lord was truly married to the backslider. His heart was so open and tender as I heard him talk about how God was drawing him. If a person wants to be reconnected to the Lord, all he or she has to do is be willing to repent and surrender their lives back to Him. Second Peter 3:9 tells us that "The Lord is not slack concerning His promise, as some men count slackness; but is longsuffering toward us, not willing that any should perish, but that all should come to repentance."

In Luke the 15th chapter, Jesus tells a powerful story (parable) of a son that strayed away from his father's house after receiving his inheritance. He squanders it all on riotous living and returns home telling his father that he had sinned against heaven, and in thy sight, and am no more worthy to be called thy son. I want to bring out two historical points that I believe will surprise many of my readers. This boy really wanted his father dead. In Jewish customs a son could not receive his inheritance until his father's death. Secondly, the Bible says the father ran to meet his son. His father had compassion and was certainly happy to see him. But again, in Jewish customs if a Jewish son lost his inheritance among Gentiles and returned home, the community would perform a ceremony, called the Kezazah. They would break a large pot in front of him and yell, "You are now cut off from your people." The father was protecting his son from the community. This was a father's unconditional love. And I believe that Jesus has an unconditional love to those that want to return back to him.

This week take out time and pray for a loved one who has fallen away from the Lord. And if by chance you are someone who has fallen away and desire to reconnect, just like the father of the prodigal son, our heavenly father, Jesus Christ, is waiting with open arms ready to welcome you home.

Lift Me Up Week 20

Spiritual Slump

Greetings Brothers and Sisters! As we walk with the Lord we sometimes find ourselves in what is known as a spiritual slump. This does not mean that you are not praying, fasting or reading God's word. Many times we find ourselves in this state when we are laboring before the Lord. It is a place where you're not able to shake off a spirit of complacency. As spiritual as we all may think we are, we are still living in this flesh. Ephesians 6:12 reminds us that as Christians we are going to wrestle, but our wrestling will not be with flesh and blood, but against principalities, against powers, against the rulers of the darkness of this world, against spiritual wickedness in high places. While we are in this spiritual state we may find ourselves growing weary, exhausted and tired. This is not a time to become discouraged, despondent or to retreat. This is the time to persevere.

Jesus knew that we would experience these encounters as we walk with Him. He tells us something very powerful in Matthew 11:28-30 that should put our minds at ease. He graciously encourages us to come unto Him. One definition of "to come" was to move into view. Once we do this, He then solves our problem by telling us exactly what we need to do to conquer this spirit of exhaustion and fatigue. He says if you are laboring and are heavy laden, come unto me and I will give you rest. He continues by saying as you learn of me you will not only find physical rest but you will also find rest for your soul. Martha was doing many things but Jesus said Mary hath chosen that good part. What was that good part? It was sitting at Jesus' feet, and hearing His word. Are you doing too many things? Do you need to stop, be still and rest in Jesus?

Many times the simplest things spoken through God's word are the antidote to our problems. Life can be complex. Spiritual warfare can be exhausting. David said it best, "When my heart is overwhelmed, lead me to the rock that is higher than I. This week, when the pressures hit, go to the rock!

_____
_____
_____
_____
_____
_____
_____
_____
_____
_____
_____
_____
_____
_____

Lift Me Up Week 21

Entertaining Angels Unaware, Really?

Greetings Brothers and Sisters! Have you ever heard anyone call a person a kook? Some of you may say yes, and others may ask, what on earth is a kook? Webster's Dictionary describes a kook as one whose ideas or actions are eccentric, fantastic, or insane. In fact, some of you may put me in that category after reading this week's Lift Me Up (smile).

In the beginning of my ministry, I held one of my first revivals in Greenville, Ohio. I departed on a very dreary day for Greenville, with one hand on the steering wheel and the other holding my GPS, a Rand McNally Road Atlas (smile). As I was driving, I noticed an older African-American women (60-65) walking very slowly. She had a small box in her hand and was walking along a highway as busy as I-70. I did something I would never encourage anyone to do then, and definitely not today. I pulled over and asked her where she was going and why she was walking on this busy highway. She told me that she was going to a small city in the country about a half hour from where I had stopped. She said as a young woman she worked for a family who owned a large home in that town. She was hoping that she would be able to get a job from them again. I was very concerned about her safety and volunteered to take her to her destination. It's funny, how ironic for me to think of how dangerous it was for her to be walking alone on the highway, and at the same time I wasn't thinking about how dangerous it was for me to be picking up a random stranger. She knew the exact location of this home. It was a beautiful older southern style home. The driveway was as long as a city block. I did not feel comfortable dropping her off in front of the house, so she got out at the edge of the driveway. Just before she got out of my car it began to rain. She got out and thanked me for the ride. I pulled away, and after driving a couple of minutes, I remembered I had an umbrella in my back seat. I turned the car around to give it to her, but she was nowhere in sight. I stayed in that area for five or ten minutes and could not find her anywhere. Hebrews 13:2 says, "Be not forgetful to entertain strangers: for thereby (some) have entertained angels unawares." You may ask me, "Why are you telling us this story Loretta? You sound like a kook." One reason I'm telling this story is because it is possible that this really could have been an angel. But the real reason I am telling this story is because the Apostle Paul wasn't wanting us to walk around acting all spooky. His real point was found in Hebrews 13:1. I believe this was his true message. "Brothers and Sisters! Continue to love one another and don't forget about strangers for some of you will entertain angels without knowing that you are entertaining angels." Whether you think I'm a kook, quack or crazy, the most important takeaway is to be kind! Your angel could be in the produce section of the grocery store or at a restaurant. But wherever they are, just make sure your love and kind Christian character are there also.

I would like to put a smile on your face this week. Play this song called Humble and Kind: By Tim McGraw.

_____
_____
_____
_____
_____
_____
_____
_____
_____
_____
_____
_____
_____
_____
_____
_____
_____
_____
_____
_____
_____
_____
_____

Lift Me Up Week 22

The Banning of the Bible

Greetings Brothers and Sisters! Some of you may know that the American Library of Association receives reports from libraries, schools, and the media on attempts to ban books in communities across the country. But what you may not know that one of the books in that list to be banned is the Bible. The association says that the Bible makes the list because of its "religious viewpoint." I'm going to be very frank here. I personally don't believe this organization would have a problem with the Bible if one name was removed from its content, and that name is Jesus.

This past Wednesday evening, I had an opportunity to give a few words of encouragement to a congregation. The scripture the Lord placed on my heart was Proverbs 18:10. The name of the Lord is a strong tower: the righteous runneth into it, and is safe. Every day for the past few weeks we have heard the horrific stories and devastation that have been brought on our country by hurricanes Harvey, Erma and Jose. The only place on this earth in which you will find total safety is in the name of Jesus. The world doesn't mind that we repeat this saying "The Name Of The Lord", but they do not want us to say the actual name of the Lord, which is Jesus.

The priests, the captain of the temple, and the Sadducees in the 3rd chapter of the book of Acts had no problem with the disciples healing the lame man at the gate called beautiful. Their problem was not the healing but rather the name that was being used for the healing. The most self-explanatory scripture about the power in the name of Jesus is found in John 14:14, If ye shall ask ANYTHING in my name, I will do it. I know we cannot use the name of Jesus openly at every venue that we attend, but if you want the attention of JESUS, you must call on His NAME. If you want supernatural DELIVERANCE, you must call on His NAME. If you want HEALING in your body, you must call on His NAME. If you want to COMBAT the devices of the enemy, you must call on His NAME. This week we cry, JESUS! JESUS! JESUS!!

_____
_____
_____
_____
_____
_____
_____
_____
_____
_____
_____
_____
_____
_____

Lift Me Up Week 23

Lord Help My Unbelief

Greetings Brothers and Sisters! This week I would like to share a few words on the subject of unbelief. I'm sure many of us have had a conversation with someone who did not believe in the existence of God nor the veracity of the word of God. Our prayer would be that they would surrender their will to the will of God. But what about Christians who allow a spirit of doubt to lie in the recesses of their heart? Especially that wife who watches her saved spouse lie in a semi-coma state for years, or the saint believing for the healing of a loved one after much prayer, only to watch them succumb to death. Perhaps you have your own experience of struggling with belief in God's promise or will. I have, in my years of being saved, questioned the Lord (respectfully) and wondered in difficult times if He was there. It was during those times when I understood the scripture in Matthew 26:41 that says, "The spirit indeed is willing, but the flesh is weak."

There is a beautiful example in Mark 9:17-25, for those who grapple with unbelief. A man brings his son to Jesus. His son has a mute spirit which torments him and makes him foam and gnash his teeth. Jesus said bring him to me. Jesus then tells the father that all things are possible to him that believeth. This gentlemen cried out with tears and said, I believe, but I am having a little struggle, will you help my unbelief. I have read this story many times and had never given much thought to this. When they brought him to Jesus, the spirit acted worse than before. We should not get aggravated or frustrated when we are believing the Lord for situations in our lives and things seem to get worse before they get better. Just as Jesus was there the entire time the spirit was acting up, He is with us every step of the way of our trials and tribulations. He has already made a way out. Amen!

I want to leave you with these words. If you are believing God for something and your faith is wavering a bit, be encouraged! Indeed He has already made a way out. And He reiterates this to us in Matthew by telling us that all things, whatsoever we shall ask in prayer, believing, we shall receive.

_____
_____
_____
_____
_____
_____
_____
_____
_____
_____
_____
_____
_____

Lift Me Up Week 24

Hot, Cold Or Lukewarm

Last year my mother's granddaughters blessed our family with one of the most memorable Thanksgiving dinners anyone could every experience. They rented a mansion outside of Nashville, TN, in the beautiful hills of Franklin. This place was exquisite. I believe one evening 29-30 members of our family stayed overnight. To top it off, the food they prepared was absolutely scrumptious. After Bishop Miller prayed for our food, I noticed a line gathering around one item in the kitchen. That item was the microwave. As wonderful as the food looked, no one wanted to eat it lukewarm. No matter how long it took, we waited patiently (well, maybe not everyone) for the use of the microwave so we could heat up the delicious presentation.

Some may think the only thing the Lord is doing to the Laodicea church in Revelations 3:15-16 is reprimanding them by telling them, "I know thy works, that thou art neither cold nor hot: I would thou wert cold or hot. So then because thou art lukewarm, and neither cold nor hot, I will spue thee out of my mouth." I believe the Lord is not just reprimanding but also showing His love for a church that has forgotten where their blessing came from. I'm sure all of us, at some point in our Christian journey, have found ourselves in a state where we didn't pray, fast or read the Bible as often as we should. I don't believe it was because we no longer loved the Lord, but rather we allowed our daily affairs to take priority. Remember when Jesus reprimands or chastises us, it is only to get our attention. He explains to the Laodicea church in the seventeenth verse why they are lukewarm. He says, "Because thou sayest, I am rich, and increased with goods, and have NEED of NOTHING." Then Jesus shows them their true colors by saying, "Knowest not that thou art wretched, and miserable, and poor, and blind, and naked." But thank goodness God doesn't reprimand us and leave us. When you go on to read the end of the story, you will see Jesus standing at the door, knocking and saying, "If any man hear my voice, and open the door, I will come in to him, and will sup with him, and he with me."

If while reading this session of Lift Me Up, you have found yourself in a lukewarm state, stop right now and speak to the Lord, (even if you have to do it silently or in your heart) and tell Him as of this moment, I am starting anew.

_____
_____
_____
_____
_____
_____
_____
_____
_____
_____

Lift Me Up Week 25

Your Adversary

We have addressed some tough topics in previous weeks, but please don't be afraid of this week's session. This week's session is a little "How To Guide" you will be able to use on your daily walk with Christ.

Have you ever heard someone ask, "How do I ward off the devil?" I can only assume they are asking, "how do I get rid of or protect myself from the devil?" In First Peter chapter 5, verse 8 Peter takes a strong stance on how we should approach warding off the enemy when he says, "Be sober, be vigilant; (meaning: clear minded and alert) because your adversary the devil, as a roaring lion, walketh about, seeking whom he may devour." Then James provides great comfort in James chapter 4, verse 7 which he says, "Resist the devil, and he will flee from us." But some may say even when I have verbally quoted this scripture, written it down and posted it in various places in my home, I still feel as if I am in constant battle with the enemy. This scripture has two parts, the (resisting) is part two. Without part one you will only be speaking words with no effect. Part one requires you to "submit (yield) yourself therefore to God." Then and only then you can resist the devil, and he will flee from you.

Jesus says this about getting rid of Satan in Matthew 4:10-11, "Then saith Jesus unto him, get thee hence, Satan: for it is written, Thou shalt worship the Lord thy God, and him only shalt thou serve." We know that Jesus always used the word against Satan, but when Jesus began to talk to Satan about WORSHIP, the Bible says, "THEN the devil leaveth him, and, behold, angels came and ministered unto him." After you have submitted to the Lord, which will provide you with the strength to resist the devil, start worshipping! Your break through to never returning to the devices of the enemy is in your worship! Then you can say, "I Have A Testimony!"

And finally, Jesus provided Luke chapter 10, verse 19 for His saints and it reads, "Behold, I give unto you power to tread on serpents and scorpions, and over ALL the power of the enemy: and NOTHING shall by any means hurt you." Submit! Resist! Worship! Then you will have power over the enemy! I hope this little "How to Guide" blesses you all week and beyond!

_____

_____

_____

_____

_____

_____

_____

Lift Me Up Week 26

Those Millennials

Greetings Brothers and Sisters! Let me talk to you about a generation of individuals who some of us know very little about. In fact, many of us don't even know who they are. And yet they live in our homes and sit on our pews. They are called the Millennials. They are generally the children of baby boomers and older Gen Xers. They are sometimes referred to as "Echo Boomers" due to a major surge in birth rates in the 1980s and 1990s. They are in the age group of 18-30, and statistics proclaim they are leaving the church in record numbers. Some of us more seasoned saints may be quick to judge and write them off by saying if they really had a desire to serve the Lord, they would be committed to church. I may be completely off in my assessment of why Millennials are not staying within the walls of the church. And if you think I have missed the mark, please pray the Lord will correct my thinking. However, after observing these vibrant and high energy young people in special services and concerts, I noticed a few things. Their music is louder, their dancing is wilder and their attire is certainly different from the attire worn by my age group. Remember statistics show they are leaving the church in record numbers. And if the statistics are accurate, I believe they are only leaving the churches that discourage them from being who they are. I don't believe it's because they don't have hearts for worship and God's word.

Joseph was seventeen when the Lord spoke to him in a dream. He would probably have been reprimanded by the pastor, elders and saints if he had shared his dream with today's church. He told his brothers and parents that they all would bow to him one day. His brothers literally hated him and his father rebuked him. This could have been the end of the story. And we may not have ever heard anything else about this young man that the Lord used mightily in our Biblical history. But thank the Lord for Joseph's father Jacob. Yes, he rebuked him, but he also asked him questions (Let us start a dialogue with this generation). Genesis 37: 10-11 reads, "He asked him, what is this dream that thou hast dreamed? Shall I and thy mother and thy brethren indeed come to bow down ourselves to thee to the earth? His brethren envied him; but his father (observed) the saying."

Let's observe (monitor, examine and watch) this Millennial generation. I believe it is our responsibility as saints of God to be an example to this very vulnerable group of young people. Let us follow the instructions of Titus the second chapter when he says to the aged men, "Be sober, grave, temperate, sound in faith, in charity, in patience. And to the aged women likewise, that we be in behaviour as becometh holiness, not false accusers, not given to much wine, teachers of good things."

Yes, we may have to reign them in a little and give them guidance. Yes, we may have to teach them to honor and respect tradition and seniority. But we also need to love, support and embrace them. If there was ever a time that our Millennials needed to be lifted up, it is now. Start the dialogue in your church.

_____

_____

_____

_____

_____

_____

_____

_____

_____

_____

_____

_____

_____

_____

_____

_____

_____

_____

_____

_____

_____

_____

_____

_____

_____

Lift Me Up Week 27

Knowing the Will of God

Greeting Brothers and Sisters! I don't know if there is anything more fulfilling than knowing you are in the will of God. I truly believe we can know His will in every aspect of our lives. James 4:15 says something so simple but yet powerful in reference to being in God's will. He first starts out by saying, "this is what you (ought) to say," James does not command or order us to say this, but he is saying you should consider saying this. "If the Lord will, we shall live, and do this, or that." The word "ought" in this passage is really quite interesting. I think most of us can understand the word a little better when used in sentences such as, "you ought to take care of yourself," or "you ought to pay your car payment." We don't have to take care of ourselves, and we don't have to pay our car payment, but there will be repercussions if we don't. I'm sure most of us have made decisions without seeking God's will. And the only thing we can say today is thank God for His grace. As I have matured in age, I find myself saying, "Lord is this your will, and if it is not please block it. Amen!"

I believe seasoned Christians should be able to discern when the Lord is speaking and how He is directing us. I know individuals who literally lean on a prophetic word from a prophet for the will of God in their life. I spoke to a young lady several years ago with two small children who told me she was moving to a particular city to be under the ministry of a renowned prophetess. I sincerely tried to dissuade her from this move as I did not feel in my spirit this was the will of God for her life. Sadly my efforts were to no avail. I believe the Lord uses men and women of God to speak into our lives, but what we choose to do with that prophetic word is totally up to us. In biblical times, the Lord used prophets to speak into the lives of his people. And I am certainly appreciative of the fivefold ministry mentioned in Ephesians 4:11 that the Lord uses to edify the church today. However, I believe if a prophet prophesies to you it is only to confirm what the Lord has already spoken into your spirit.

I want to close by saying, after you feel you are in the will of the Lord make sure that the direction you believe the Lord is taking you concurs with His word. His will, will never contradict His word.

_____

_____

_____

_____

_____

_____

_____

_____

_____

_____

_____

_____

Lift Me Up Week 28

Regret, The Tormentor

Greetings Brothers and Sisters! This week I would like to speak on a subject that I pray my readers will understand and receive total victory over. I would like to talk about the pain of regret. I don't know if there is anything more haunting than remembering something you did or said that you wish you could take back or erase from your mind. The Apostle Paul tries to help us by telling us to forget those things that are behind. And yet the enemy will continue to bring up things the Lord has forgiven us for. The Lord uses a metaphor to describe how far our weights and sins are from Him. He tells us in Micah 7:19, "He will have compassion upon us; he will subdue our iniquities; and thou wilt cast all their sins into the depths of the sea." Every now and then the devil would love for us to put on our invisible scuba diving equipment to bring forth things that the Lord has forgiven us for. But I want you to understand that no matter how deep you dive you will not find any of your repented sins, for the blood at the cross has erased them all. Hebrews 8:12 says, "For I will be merciful to their unrighteousness, and their sins and their iniquities will I remember no more."

There was a disciple who regretted saying something in Matthew 26:75. This disciple found himself weeping bitterly over what he had done. "Jesus told Peter before the cock crows, thou will deny me three times. Peter said unto him, though I should die with thee, yet will I not deny thee (Special note: all the disciples said the same thing)." This next part is very interesting. After Peter denies Jesus three times, Jesus turns and looks at Peter. The Bible does not say that Jesus reminds Peter of what he said, it is Peter who remembers the words that the Lord spoke to him. Jesus went to the cross for the sins of the world, it didn't matter that Peter had just denied him, lied and cursed, because in a short period of time all of Peter's sins would be forgiven, never to be remembered again.

There are many things in this life that we all want and need to remember, but when it comes to our regret, let's do like Jesus and never remember them again. No more deep sea diving for regrets. This week, unless you're diving for joy, love and peace in knowing God already forgave you and forgot, hang up the scuba gear!

_____

_____

_____

_____

_____

_____

_____

_____

_____

_____

_____

Lift Me Up Week 29

What Did You Call Me?

Greetings Brothers and Sisters! How would you feel if you spoke to someone you loved and respected, but they would not acknowledge your presence while you were speaking to them? And when they finally spoke to you, they called you a name that was belittling. I can imagine how an unsaved person would respond. But hopefully, as Christians, we would attempt to talk to this person and try to understand the motive behind their behavior. This actually happened to a woman in the Bible. She was able to move beyond an offensive moment to receive an eternal blessing.

Jesus wants her story told. He starts out by saying "Behold," in other words, "observe and notice this woman." It is obvious to me she knew who Jesus was beyond just the rumors of His miraculous ability to heal or beyond seeing the crowds gather around Him. I say this because she doesn't call him Jesus, but she refers to him as "thou Son of David." She knew this was the coming Messiah and that He was the deliverer. This woman had a situation in her life that she knew only the deliverer could resolve. She had a daughter who was not just vexed by a devil that continuously annoyed and agitated her, but this evil spirit was grievously vexing her and causing her pain and anguish. This story was told in the twentieth chapter of Matthew. Is it possible that she could have heard how Jesus, in Matthew 4:1, was led up of the Spirit into the wilderness to be tempted of the devil? This is just speculation, but is it possible that she felt if anyone could understand her situation it was Jesus, the man who resisted the devil. Whatever the motivation, this woman made it a point to activate her faith and get what she needed from Jesus no matter what. This woman did not care that the disciples told Jesus to send her away. She did not care that Jesus did not speak to her. She didn't even care that Jesus referred to her as a dog. She even agreed with his analogy that insinuated she was a dog. She did not care what they said or did to her so long as when she got back home her daughter was healed. And when you read the conclusion of her story you will find out that Jesus healed her daughter that very hour. This Canaanite woman would not allow her faith to be interrupted by the offense.

When you are seeking the Lord, you can't allow anything or anyone to hinder you from receiving what has been promised to you. Who cares if they roll their eyes at you? Who cares if they talk about you? As humans we experience hurt, broken-hearts, disappointment, rejection and so much more. But never allow a MOMENT of offense, pain, rejection or regret to allow you to lose faith and miss an ETERNAL blessing.

_____
_____
_____
_____

Lift Me Up Week 30

Let's Go To Church!

Greetings Brothers and Sisters! Let's go to church! I am amazed at the statistics regarding Christians who do not attend church regularly. A new report by Barna states there are those who "love Jesus, but not the church." This crowd shares a lot of core beliefs with their churchgoing neighbors; nearly all of them (around 95%) believe in only one God, that He is everywhere, and that He is the "all-powerful, all-knowing, perfect creator of the universe who rules the world today." And 89 percent of them are committed to Jesus. But they have lost faith in the church," said Roxanne Stone, editor-in-chief of Barna Group.

I personally have to dispute one portion of a statement that the Barna report seems to emphatically believe about this group of Christians. They say that 89 percent of them are committed to Jesus. I don't know how you can commit to Jesus and separate from the church. The scripture that I heard quoted often by my pastor, the late Everett Keller, growing up about attending church service was Hebrews 10:25, "Not forsaking the assembling of ourselves together, as the manner of some is; but exhorting one another: and so much the more, as ye see the day approaching." His encouragement to us was to attend service every time the church doors were open. So, as a young new Christian coming up, I found myself attending Tuesday and Thursday night Bible study, Sunday school, Sunday morning worship service and Sunday evening service. Most churches probably don't have that many services today, but as new converts, we didn't complain.

I would like to share with you a statement quoted by the great King David of Israel about going to The House of the Lord. Like many of you I have read this scripture many times over and over again. But I read it a few months ago and shared this revelation with our church. Most of us think David was glad, happy, cheerful, overjoyed, gratified and excited when he went into the house of the Lord. However, if you examine his statement carefully, David's excitement was in reference to something else. David felt excited when someone said to him, "David let's go to the house of the Lord." He was excited that someone suggested they go, not because they were there. If David felt this way just hearing someone say "Let's go to church," can you imagine what David was doing when he got there? We already know how he responded when the Ark of The Lord returned to Israel. If he danced before the Lord (not naked) with just a linen ephod (loincloth, kilt, or apron) on, and he was overjoyed when someone just suggested going to the house of the Lord, can you imagine David's excitement and radical praise once he stepped into the doors of the temple?

This week I encourage those of you who have been watching your favorite TV minister on the big screen to turn it off, get dressed and assemble with your fellow brothers and sisters in Christ. And to those of us who go every Sunday, maybe it's time for us to do more outreach. Your invitation to a friend or stranger to come to the House of the Lord with you, may be the very thing they need to get them excited and motivated to walk through the doors of the church. This week, "Let's go to church!"

Lift Me Up Week 31

The Definition of Miserable

Greetings Brothers and Sisters! Please allow me to be a little lengthier this week with Lift Me Up because of the urgency of my message. I have only spoken once from 1 Corinthians 15:13-19, and if you have any inkling of doubt about the return of our Lord and Savior Jesus Christ, I pray that this week's Lift Me Up will remove any pessimism inside of you.

The Apostle Paul in this passage describes the word miserable better than any modern dictionary that we have available today. People give all kinds of excuses for why they are miserable. The Apostle Paul gives only one. His basic definition of miserable is believing that there is no resurrection (Please read 1 Corinthians 15:13-19). As he elaborates, he emphasizes how our faith is in vain if we believe this erroneous doctrine of no resurrection. He makes this declaration in the 19th verse by saying, "If in this life only we have hope in Christ, we are of all men most miserable." Let me paraphrase, if after getting baptized and being filled with the Holy Spirit, living a life of Godliness, walking upright before the Lord, and our life literally ends at the grave, your life has been miserable. However, our story does not end there. Titus 1:2 tells us that we have hope of eternal life before the world began, and that God CANNOT lie.

The story below will make you appreciate the fact
that you know without a doubt that you have made
your calling and election sure.

*As Vice President, George Bush represented the
U.S. at the funeral of former Soviet leader Leonid
Brezhnev in 1982. Bush was deeply moved by a
silent protest carried out by Brezhnev's widow. She
stood motionless by the coffin until seconds before it
was closed. Then, just as the soldiers touched the
lid, Brezhnev's wife performed an act of great
courage and hope, a gesture that must surely rank
as one of the most profound acts of civil
disobedience ever committed: She reached down
and made the sign of the cross on her husband's
chest. There in the citadel of secular, atheistic
power, the wife of the man who had run it all hoped
that her husband was wrong. She hoped that there
was another life, and that life was best represented
by Jesus who died on the cross, and that the same
Jesus might yet have mercy on her husband. Gary
Thomas, in Christianity Today, October 3, 1994, p.
26*

We, who have a deep knowledge of the word of
God, understand that it takes more than making a
cross sign across the chest of an individual to assure
salvation. And it is extremely heartbreaking that
Mrs. Brezhnev was not able to convince her
husband that Jesus was the Lord of the cross. I'm
sure that if she could have convinced him of this,
the Soviet Union would be a different country
today. I personally wonder if there were times that

he looked at his wife and said "Almost thou persuaded me to be a Christian."

When we take our last breath on this earth, when our purpose for God's kingdom has been fulfilled and when our race has finally come to an end, we won't need anyone to form the sign of the cross on our chests. For we know and believe that if we have hope in Christ and His death and resurrection, we have been saved by His grace, filled with the Holy Spirit and lived upright and holy Christian lives, when the final trumpet sounds all will be well with our souls.

_____

_____

_____

_____

_____

_____

_____

_____

_____

_____

_____

_____

_____

_____

_____

_____

_____

_____

Lift Me Up Week 32

Get Rich Quick Plan

Greetings Brothers and Sisters! Every now and then the Lord will lay a subject on my heart that may not seem very spiritual but will hopefully edify my readers. I am certain the majority of you have had someone approach you about a "Get Rich Quick" opportunity. The plan is to obtain high rates of return for a small investment. These "opportunities" usually require you to continue to recruit individuals in order to receive the financial benefits of the "opportunity." The terminology for these schemes are called pyramids. In 2008 we began to hear the horrific stories of investors investing their money into companies which were nothing more than Ponzi schemes. This is where existing investors are compensated by the contribution of new investors, with many of these new investors losing their entire life savings.

I have a better opportunity for those of you that want to be blessed abundantly. The difference between what I will share with you and what a Ponzi scheme offers, is my opportunity guarantees you will reap abundantly. Based on biblical principles, when we sow, we should expect the windows of heaven to open up so we can reap blessings that there shall not be room enough to receive. But did you know that he that hath pity (compassion sympathy concern empathy) upon the poor will not only be blessed of the Lord but will also be paid back? The Lord literally says if you will help the poor, consider it a loan. Proverbs 19:17 reads, "He that hath pity upon the poor lendeth unto the Lord; and that which he hath given will he pay him again."

There are a number of scriptures encouraging Christians to help the poor. Please allow me to share a few with you. NIV Proverbs: 22:9 reads, "The generous will themselves be blessed, for they share their food with the poor." NIV Luke 14:13-15 reads, "Then Jesus said to his host, When you give a luncheon or dinner, do not invite your friends, your brothers or sisters, your relatives, or your rich neighbors; if you do, they may invite you back and so you will be repaid. But when you give a banquet, invite the poor, the crippled, the lame, the blind and you will be blessed. Although they cannot repay you, you will be repaid at the resurrection of the righteous."

I want to close with this last verse. 1 John 3:17 says, "But whoso hath this world's good, and seeth his brother have need, and shutteth up his bowels of compassion from him, how dwelleth the love of God in him?" I must explain why this is one of my favorite scriptures on taking care of the poor. John does not want you to give to the poor if it is not in your heart, and he does not want you to do it because you feel guilty. He's actually asking us a question by saying, How dwelleth the love of God in you if you see a brother in need and have no compassion for him? Ponzi schemes are full of personal ambition and, often times, greed. However, when it comes to this opportunity of abundance, it is about making sure your heart and intentions are pure.

This week please pray about opening your heart to those who are in need. And don't feel like you have to go donate thousands of dollars to a not for profit. You can start small with something as simple as donating food, or purchasing a warm meal for someone on the street. When this becomes part of your lifestyle, watch how God finds ways to bless you beyond your wildest imagination. You don't need a pyramid scheme, you simply need a pure heart to help those in need. God bless you.

_____

_____

_____

_____

_____

_____

_____

_____

_____

_____

_____

_____

_____

_____

Lift Me Up Week 33

Just Ask

Greetings Brothers and Sisters! This is my week of confession. I have been so frustrated at myself for the past few weeks for not petitioning the Lord on something I have desired for the past few years. I realized last week my reason for not receiving what I desired had nothing to do with the Lord, but with me. I consider myself a woman of faith, so it was not my lack of faith that was hindering the receipt of my blessing. I was asking, and not receiving because my method of asking was amiss. I was doing what James told us not to do in James 4:3. There was also another problem with my prayer, and that was whether or not I deserved what I was requesting from the Lord. Matthew 7:7-8 says, "Ask, and it shall be given you; seek, and ye shall find; knock, and it shall be opened unto you. 8 For every one that asketh receiveth; and he that seeketh findeth; and to him that knocketh it shall be opened." Just in case you get a little confused with the order of asking, seeking and knocking, just remember the word A-S-K. It's really easy to ask, seek and knock, but we must have the right motive for our request.

I had to talk to myself by saying, "Loretta, are you really delighting yourself in the Lord?" I answered "yes," and said "Lord, I believe with all my heart that I am walking upright before you and pleasing you." And the Lord spoke back to me through His word by telling me, "If you are, I will give you the desires of your heart." What I desired involved the decision of another individual. I sent a letter to this person and immediately received a favorable response.

Remember as you're asking, seeking and knocking, no good thing will the Lord withhold from them that walk in integrity. We all need something from the Lord, and he's willing to provide when we are obedient. What will be your ASK?

_____

_____

_____

_____

_____

_____

_____

_____

_____

_____

_____

_____

_____

_____

_____

_____

_____

_____

Lift Me Up Week 34

No One Knows the Day or Hour

Greetings Brothers and Sisters! Maybe you have heard messages in the past that we (Christians) should not get caught up in the goods of this world because of the soon coming of the Lord Jesus Christ. In fact, there was a religious organization founded by William Miller that ignited one of the largest movements in American history. Miller believed that the rapture would take place on October 22, 1844. His 100,000 followers sold all their worldly possessions. When the rapture failed to occur, the Millerites were devastated. Sadly to say they would not have been disappointed had they taken heed to Matthew 25:13 that says, "Watch therefore, for ye know neither the day nor the hour wherein the Son of man cometh." After reading this story about William Miller and his followers, I thought it was interesting that they sold all of their worldly possessions. Logic would say, give everything away if you really believed the rapture was going to take place. I have a funny feeling that some of these folk did an Ananias, and Sapphira on Mr. Miller and his followers (Read Acts 5:1-11), smile.

I want to encourage anyone who's putting anything off for fear of the rapture. Get your degree, buy your new home, get married, have that second child, go on that European Cruise, start writing your book, add that addition to your home, start your new business, build that new church, for the Bible tells us to occupy until He comes. And it also says to comfort one another with these words, "For the Lord himself shall descend from heaven with a shout, with the voice of the archangel, and with the trump of God: and the dead in Christ shall rise first: Then we which are alive and remain shall be caught up together with them in the clouds, to meet the Lord in the air: and so shall we ever be with the Lord." One day we will walk streets paved with gold with our Lord and savior Jesus Christ. But before that gold is used for pavement, we might as well enjoy a couple pieces of jewelry (smile). What have you been putting off? "Thy Kingdom come, thy will be done, on earth as it is in Heaven." This week I challenge you to start living life to the fullest and enjoy some heaven on earth!

_____

_____

_____

_____

_____

_____

_____

_____

_____

_____

_____

_____

_____

Lift Me Up Week 35

Hindrances

Greetings Brothers and Sisters! I believe this week's Lift Me Up may be a little difficult for some of my readers to receive. The subject is hindrances; the thing or individual that causes delays in your ability to progress in your spiritual life. Hindrances can also be described as obstacles which hold or slow you down. Some of us may remember when we were saved and surrendered everything to God. We would not do anything without His consent. We took Tye Tribbett's song "No Way I Can Make It Without You" literally! The song says, "I can't even sing my song, I wouldn't know right from wrong, I can't even comb my hair, can't even look or stare, I can't even walk my walk, not even talk my talk." The reason I say some of my readers may not be able to receive this week's Lift Me Up is because when it comes to certain things or people, Tye Tribbett's lyrics fly out the window and in flies our own desires. We all know that person or that thing that hinders us from drawing closer to the Lord, but we're just not ready to remove him, her, them or it from our life.

When the Apostle Paul addresses the Galatians in chapter 5, verse 7, he first compliments them by saying, "Ye did run well." The (did) lets us know that they had gotten off track and were no longer following the path the Lord had set before them. Paul had a question for them that he wanted them to answer. He asked, "who did hinder you that ye should not obey the truth?" In the third chapter he is not shy with his words. Paul says, "not only are you hindered, but who has bewitched you?" What he is asking is "who has control over you?" We can all sing collectively "I Surrender All" but words to a song are just words if we don't apply them to our lives.

The eternal promises of Christ are so much greater than the temporary pleasures people and things of this world can bring. This week, let's be intentional in ridding ourselves of the obstacles in our way so that we may "run well" and into the purpose God has ordained for our lives. You just may find that once you let the hindrance go, God has something greater on the other side.

_____

_____

_____

_____

_____

_____

_____

_____

_____

_____

_____

_____

_____

Lift Me Up Week 36

A Long and Prosperous Life

Greetings Brothers and Sisters! I was so inspired
and lifted up with Psalms 34:12 that I decided to
share it with my readers this week. The psalmist
asks a question that stopped me in my tracks. He
asks, "What man is he that desireth life, and loveth
many days, that he may see good?" The new living
translation asks it this way, "Does anyone want to
live a life that is long and prosperous?" My reaction
was sign me up!! Me!! Me!! Pick me! I want to be
that person (smile)! This verse alone is saying
something so powerful that if you grasp it, it could
literally turn your life around in seconds.

The very first thing you must do is desire life. It
breaks my heart to hear a Christian say they live a
miserable life. Jesus tells us that He came not to
only give us life but to give it to us more
abundantly. If you don't desire life, stop reading
right now and sincerely ask the Lord to give you a
desire for life. The second thing is to love life many
days. Psalms 90:10 tells us that we are to live 70
years and if we are strong 80 years. We all know
many who have surpassed these years. No matter
how many years we live in Christ, the life we live
should be filled with glorious years. The scripture
closes by saying if you desire life, you will love
your days and your days will be good.
Once you desire life and learn to love life, the next
two verses are the key to having and maintaining

that long, prosperous life. Psalms 34:13-14 reads, "Then keep your tongue from speaking evil and your lips from telling lies! Turn away from evil and do good. Search for peace, and work to maintain it."

In closing, let us pray this prayer: God help us speak nothing but positivity this week and guide us in our search for peace. Then we will desire and experience a prosperous life full of glorious years! Amen!

_____
_____
_____
_____
_____
_____
_____
_____
_____
_____
_____
_____
_____
_____
_____
_____
_____
_____
_____
_____

Lift Me Up Week 37

Stay On Your Path

I count it a joy to wake up and say, "Thank you Lord for another day." Each morning we should give the Lord praise for another day of life. Psalm 16:11 reads, "Thou wilt shew me the path of life..."

A path is a trail that has been prepared for individuals to get from one point to the next. There is something one must do on a trail which is vital to survival. It can mean the difference between safety and danger or life and death. That one thing is to always follow the signs to avoid getting lost. The Lord has mapped out signs throughout His word for each one of us to utilize on our daily Christian journey. If you stay on this path you will see the trail the Lord has prepared specifically for you. If you are one of those individuals that has strayed off the path, remember Jesus tells us in Hebrews 13:5, "I will NEVER leave thee nor forsake thee." This passage reassures us that if you have strayed off the path, it isn't too late to get back to safety. Our Savior is there to guide you back to His plan for your life.

_____

_____

_____

_____

_____

Lift Me Up Week 38

Be Not Troubled

If you watch local or cable news stations, you may have, at one point in time or another, heard the anchors address a subject that is no doubt unnerving to all listeners. The subject is war. No matter how saved you are there is something about war that makes most of us uncomfortable. And yet, we know the Bible speaks of wars in the last days. I want you to read this passage of scripture out loud: Matthew 24:6, And ye shall hear of wars and rumors of wars: for all these things must come to pass, but the end is not yet. Did you read what Matthew said? He said you will HEAR about wars. Simply hearing about it doesn't mean it's going to happen. He continues by saying some of these wars you are hearing about are RUMORS. If you are familiar with Matthew 24:6, you will notice that I intentionally left out the most important phrase in this passage. Matthew also says, SEE THAT YE BE NOT TROUBLED: I am not telling you that we are not going to experience wars. Given the state of domestic and global affairs I would be foolish to think we are exempt from potential war.

I realize after writing the above paragraph that there are readers that still battle the fear of our country going into war and possibly it reaching our shores. But as Christians we cannot live our lives fearful nor worrying as to whether or not North Korea, Syria, Iran or any other country that displays hostility towards us will attack us at any time. Additionally, we should not live in a constant state of fear in general. If you are fearful, I would like to encourage you to take heed to the Apostle Paul's writings to Timothy in Second Timothy 1:1-7. He inspires Timothy by first calling him my dearly beloved son. He tells him that I remember you in my prayers day and night. He reminisces of their last visit by saying, I remember your tears the last time we were together and that there is joy in my heart about seeing you again. He also talks about his genuine and sincere faith that he received from his mother and grandmother. He then tells him to stir up the gift that is inside of him. After the Apostle Paul showers Timothy with words of praise, he drops a bombshell on his dearly beloved son that I don't believe Timothy was expecting. Paul says this to this powerful man of faith in verse 7. "For God hath not given us the spirit of fear," I personally believe that Timothy battled fear. Paul wants Timothy to also know that it is a SPIRIT of fear. He goes on by saying to Timothy, "but of power, and of love, and of a sound mind." He had to add love for the Apostle Paul knew that it is love that casteth out fear. Psalm 118:6 The Lord is on my side; I will not fear: what can man do unto me?

_____

_____

_____

_____

_____

Lift Me Up Week 39

We're Not Afraid

Greetings Brothers and Sisters! This week, I am continuing with the theme of last week's topic, "Be Not Troubled." I hope that you are praying daily for the many tragedies that have befallen our cities, our country and the world. The one thing that you must recognize is that the enemy wants to put a spirit of fear upon the people of God. If we, the church, display a spirit of fear, where does the world go for comfort? Matthew 6:34 in the NIV says, "Therefore do not worry about tomorrow, for tomorrow will worry about itself. Each day has enough trouble of its own."

Psalm 23:4 is our solace. "Yea, though I walk through the valley of the shadow of death, I will fear no evil: for thou art with me; thy rod and thy staff they comfort me." The only way to get out of the valley of the shadow of death is to keep walking. Remember that this valley can also be an attack on your mind. This verse identifies the threat as the shadow of death. A shadow is an outline, a silhouette. It is not real. The adversary wants us to be fearful of death when we gather in a large crowd, a shopping mall, our schools, universities and even our places of worship. It is time to let the enemy know like Job, that the Lord has put a spiritual hedge around you and that your trust is in God and, "I will not be afraid of what man can do unto me." Psalm 56:11.

Don't let the tragedies of the world stunt your life. Of course we must be wise and watch and pray daily, and often pray continually throughout the day. But don't stop living life for fear of death. I speak peace, comfort, joy and fullness of life over all my readers this week. God is with us!

Lift Me Up Week 40

The Heart Fixer

Greetings Brothers and Sisters! This week I would like to talk about the heart. Our physical heart is a muscular organ that pumps blood through your body. Your heart is at the center of your circulatory system. This system consists of a network of blood vessels, such as arteries, veins, and capillaries. These blood vessels carry blood to and from all areas of your body. And we all understand that there is no life without the heart. But there is also another heart that should beat louder than the physical heart, and that is the heart that is after God. There is no life without a physical heart and there is no life without a spiritual heart.

Before David asked the Lord to create in him a clean heart in Psalms 51, he first said, "Have mercy on me oh God." He continues his prayer with, "Create in me a clean heart," and David understands that it is impossible to have a clean heart and his spirit is not right with the Lord. His next request is, "renew a right spirit within me." In that moment, it didn't matter to David who in his past had hurt or disappointed him, he wanted a right spirit within himself. David had a legitimate petition for his next two prayers. If you're familiar with the story of David, you know he committed atrocious sins against God. Even though he had a heart of repentance, he did not want to take advantage of God's Mercy and His Grace. His next two prayers are, "Cast me not away from thy presence;" and "take not thy Holy Spirit from me."

The heart is a tricky thing. Even with our best intentions, sometimes there are things buried deep inside which we don't even realize are shaping our thoughts, our words and our actions. No matter how wonderful we may think we are, and no matter how beautiful or "well put together, we may appear on the outside, every now and then we need to get a "checkup" on our spiritual heart just like we do an annual "checkup" on our physical heart. But there's no need to visit a doctor. Simply pray, "Create in me a clean heart oh Lord and renew a right spirit within me."

_____

_____

_____

_____

_____

_____

_____

_____

_____

_____

_____

_____

_____

_____

Lift Me Up Week 41

True Forgiveness

The Apostle Paul says something so inspiring in Philippians 3:13. And if we would apply this simple yet powerful action to our lives, we would experience overwhelming victory. He begins his declaration by saying "This ONE thing I do." This powerful man of God is not giving us a five or ten step program or a list of impossible rules to follow, but simply one thing. He goes on to say he has one word for us to focus on and that is "FORGET." In essence, Paul was saying if anyone had a right to remember the terrible things he had done to others and had been done to him, it was him. I have heard ministers make this statement, (I personally do not share their sentiments), "You have not forgiven if you can remember the negative things individuals have done or said about you." It would be wonderful if we could erase every negative offense from our mind with a magic "forgiveness means you forget" serum. As nice as this sounds and as wealthy as I would be if I could create it, the flesh we battle daily will not oblige us to do so. With God's spirit residing in us we may not be able to forget everything but we CAN and MUST forgive everyone. The Apostle Paul had this to say before he instructed us to FORGET, "Brethren, I count not myself to have apprehended." In other words, I don't understand or perceive everything, but if I want to be used of God, if I want to continue writing under the unction of the Holy Spirit, I must forget the things that were done to me and the unjust transgressions I have done to others. God wants to use you as He used Paul! Today is your day to let the past go and move forward into your divine purpose!

Isaiah 43:18 Remember ye not the former things, neither consider the things of old.

_____
_____
_____
_____
_____
_____
_____
_____
_____
_____
_____
_____
_____
_____
_____
_____
_____
_____
_____
_____
_____

Lift Me Up Week 42

W W J D?

Greeting Brothers and Sisters! Most of us remember this popular phrase from the 90s, What Would Jesus Do, "WWJD"? The phrase was associated with an athletic wristband which became a popular accessory for members of Christian youth groups across the globe. I even noticed mention of the phrase in one of Tyler Perry's movies. The WWJD phenomenon began in 1990 when a youth group leader at Calvary Reformed Church in Holland, Michigan, named Janie Tinklenberg, began a grassroots movement to help the teenagers in her group remember the phrase. It spread worldwide among Christian youth. This is an interesting note, the phrase did not come from Ms. Tinklenberg. It actually came from a book written by Charles Sheldon in 1896 called "In His Steps: What Would Jesus Do?" I encourage all of my readers to pull up "The Fascinating Story of How the 'What Would Jesus Do' Slogan Came About." You will also discover that Mr. Sheldon was a firm supporter of gender and racial equality and was one of the few white ministers of the day to not only allow, but openly invite, black people to become members of his church. Don't forget this was the late 1800's and that type of unity across racial and gender lines was unheard of, but then again, his motto was "What Would Jesus Do".

If you're really wondering what would Jesus do, I found a woman in the Bible who knew more about him than anyone; his mother, Mary. Mary gave the biblical answer for this question. She tells her son in John 2:1-5 that they have no wine for the wedding in Cana. Jesus says to her, "Woman, what have I to do with thee mine hour is not yet come." He was saying that the hour to show himself as Messiah King of the Jews had not yet arrived. Mary is not offended by the words of her son. Mary makes this very clear by telling the servants, "Whatsoever he saith unto you, DO IT." See Mary had been around Jesus long enough to have witnessed on many occasions that when you do what He says and when you pattern your walk after His, you get supernatural results.

When faced with difficult decisions or challenging interactions, we don't always need a deep word or long prayer. Sometimes, we simply need to pause and ask ourselves, "What would Jesus do?" This week, before you respond to a rude person at work, before you fall to pieces because your finances seem to be falling short, before you answer the phone to hear from the neighborhood gossiper, before you make any decision that has great implications for your future, stop and ask yourself like the teens from youth groups across the country in the 90s, "WWJD?

_____

_____

_____

Lift Me Up Week 43

The Comforter

Greetings Brothers and Sisters! Because of three devastating losses in one week, I found myself reaching out and comforting several brothers and sisters in the Lord. I believe it is our responsibility as saints to lift up, encourage and console one another when we are going through trying times. When you read Second Corinthians 1:3-4 you will see that God is a God of all comfort. In this passage, He explains why He gives us comfort. He says, "I comfort you so that you will be able to comfort them which are in any trouble."

It is so encouraging to read Deuteronomy 31:8 which reads, "Do not be afraid or discouraged, for the Lord will personally go ahead of you. He will be with you; he will neither fail you nor abandon you." And Psalm 27:5, "For in the time of trouble he shall hide me in his pavilion: in the secret of his tabernacle shall he hide me; he shall set me up upon a rock." And finally, Psalm 61:2, which reads, "From the end of the earth will I cry unto thee, when my heart is overwhelmed: lead me to the rock that is higher than I."

In times of grief, sorrow, loss, disappointment, heartbreak, pain and or despair, we as humans may not always have the perfect words to uplift one another. It is in these times we should allow the powerful word of God to bring peace, love, joy, reassurance and comfort. And in the midst of reading and sharing God's Holy Scriptures to encourage your fellow brother and or sister in Christ, you may just find God's sweet peace and everlasting comfort coming also to you.

This week, take time to dig a little deeper into God's word and allow it to "LIFT YOU UP!"

_____

_____

_____

_____

_____

_____

_____

_____

_____

_____

_____

_____

_____

_____

_____

_____

_____

_____

_____

_____

_____

_____

Lift Me Up Week 43

His Mercy Endureth Forever!

Greetings Brothers and Sisters! There may be a lot of things we don't know or understand about the Bible. But after you read the 136th chapter of Psalms in this week's "Lift Me Up," you will know without a doubt that God's mercy endureth forever. There are 26 verses in this chapter and they all end with this phase, "for his mercy endureth forever." I am in awe of this Psalm. It truly shows God's unwavering love to all that give Him praise. You don't need a "Matthew Henry's Commentator" or a "Strong's Exhaustive Concordance" to understand the meaning of this chapter. We have less than two weeks before we celebrate Thanksgiving. Let's start early with our praise and worship to our Lord and Savior Jesus Christ by reading a Psalm that simply tells us that if we want the Lord to continue loving us, we must give him praise:

Psalms 136
>   1. O give thanks unto the Lord; for he is good: for his mercy endureth forever.
>   2. O give thanks unto the God of gods: for his mercy endureth forever.
>   3. O give thanks to the Lord of lords: for his mercy endureth forever.
>   4. To him who alone doeth great wonders: for his mercy endureth forever.
>   5. To him that by wisdom made the heavens: for his mercy endureth forever.

6. To him that stretched out the earth above the waters: for his mercy endureth forever.
7. To him that made great lights: for his mercy endureth forever:
8. The sun to rule by day: for his mercy endureth forever:
9. The moon and stars to rule by night: for his mercy endureth forever.
10. To him that smote Egypt in their firstborn: for his mercy endureth forever:
11. And brought out Israel from among them: for his mercy endureth forever:
12. With a strong hand, and with a stretched out arm: for his mercy endureth forever.
13. To him which divided the Red sea into parts: for his mercy endureth forever:
14. And made Israel to pass through the midst of it: for his mercy endureth forever:
15. But overthrew Pharaoh and his host in the Red sea: for his mercy endureth forever.
16. To him which led his people through the wilderness: for his mercy endureth forever.
17. To him which smote great kings: for his mercy endureth forever:
18. And slew famous kings: for his mercy endureth forever:
19. Sihon king of the Amorites: for his mercy endureth forever:
20. And Og the king of Bashan: for his mercy endureth forever:
21. And gave their land for an inheritance: for his mercy endureth forever:

22. Even an heritage unto Israel his servant: for his mercy endureth forever.
23. Who remembered us in our low estate: for his mercy endureth forever:
24. And hath redeemed us from our enemies: for his mercy endureth forever.
25. Who giveth food to all flesh: for his mercy endureth forever.
26. O give thanks unto the God of heaven: for his mercy endureth forever.

Lift Me Up Week 45

Thanksgiving Trivia

Greeting Brothers and Sisters! This week will not be my usual writings, but rather a fun read for you and your family to reflect on the history of this wonderful Thanksgiving celebration. Please enjoy a little Thanksgiving trivia. And no matter where you are celebrating this week, remember to give thanks to the Lord.

1. The first Thanksgiving was held in the autumn of 1621 and included 50 Pilgrims and 90 Wampanoag Indians and lasted three days. Many historians believe that only five women were present at that first Thanksgiving, as many women settlers didn't survive that difficult first year in the U.S.

2. Thanksgiving didn't become a national holiday until over 200 years later! Sarah Josepha Hale, the woman who actually wrote the classic song "Mary Had a Little Lamb," convinced President Lincoln in 1863 to make Thanksgiving a national holiday, after writing letters for 17 years campaigning for this to happen.

3. No turkey on the menu at the first Thanksgiving: Historians say that no turkey was served at the first Thanksgiving! What was on the menu? Deer or venison, ducks, geese, oysters, lobster, eel and fish. They probably ate pumpkins, but no pumpkin pies.

They also didn't eat mashed potatoes or cranberry relish, but they probably ate cranberries.

4. No forks at the first Thanksgiving! The first Thanksgiving was eaten with spoons and knives — but no forks! That's right, forks weren't even introduced to the Pilgrims until 10 years later and weren't a popular utensil until the 18th century.

5. Thanksgiving is the reason for TV dinners! In 1953, Swanson had so much extra turkey (260 tons) that a salesman told them they should package it onto aluminum trays with other sides like sweet potatoes — and the first TV dinner was born!

6. Thanksgiving was almost a fast — not a feast! The early settlers gave thanks by praying and abstaining from food, which is what they planned on doing to celebrate their first harvest, that is, until the Wampanoag Indians joined them and (lucky for us!) turned their fast into a three-day feast!

7. Presidential pardon of a turkey: Each year, the president of the U.S pardons a turkey and spares it from being eaten for Thanksgiving dinner. The first turkey pardon ceremony started with President Truman in 1947. President Obama pardoned a 45-pound turkey named Courage, who has flown to Disneyland and served as Grand Marshal of the park's Thanksgiving Day parade!

8. Why is Thanksgiving the fourth Thursday in November? President Abe Lincoln said

Thanksgiving would be the fourth Thursday in November, but in 1939 President Roosevelt moved it up a week hoping it would help the shopping season during the Depression era. It never caught on and it was changed back two years later.

9. The Macy's Thanksgiving Day Parade began in 1924 with 400 employees marching from Convent Ave to 145th street in New York City. No large balloons were at this parade, as it featured only live animals from Central Park Zoo.

Lift Me Up Week 46

Immanuel, God With Us

Greetings Brothers and Sisters! This week I would like to focus on the book of Isaiah. This book gives us foreknowledge of the coming of Christ. One passage in particular that many of us are familiar with is found in Isaiah 9:6, "For unto us a child is born, unto us a son is given: and the government shall be upon his shoulder: and his name shall be called Wonderful, Counsellor, The mighty God, The everlasting Father, The Prince of Peace." Another one is found in Isaiah 7:14, "Therefore the Lord himself shall give you a sign; Behold, a virgin shall conceive, and bear a son, and shall call his name Immanuel." Can you imagine how fascinating this must have been for the prophet that penned these words about a child that would become Immanuel, God with us?

The writer in Isaiah 40:28-29 (I say the writer because there was more than one writer in Isaiah) wants us to know two very important things about this awesome God that we serve. He asks these questions, "hast thou not known, hast thou not heard, that the everlasting God, the Lord, the Creator of the ends of the earth, fainteth not, neither is weary? He is telling us that the God that we serve can handle any situation in our life. And while we are petitioning Him He will not faint nor be weary of our continuous request to Him.

This week's LMU is a very personal one for me. I am praying and calling on the name of the Lord for six friends who need a divine intervention from God. They all need a supernatural touch from the hem of His garment. Many of us have been praying for these beautiful women of God. And I know the Lord is intervening on our behalf. The woman in Matthew the 9th chapter was healed by her faith, for the Lord said, "Daughter, be of good comfort; thy faith hath made thee whole." Please pray with me for these precious women of God as the Lord increases their faith during this very difficult time of their lives. And as their faith increases, let our intercessions on their behalf increase. For we know our righteous and awesome God, the creator of the earth will not grow weary or faint at our requests, but will intervene in each of their situations. What a mighty God we serve!

_____
_____
_____
_____
_____
_____
_____
_____
_____
_____
_____

Lift Me Up Week 47

My Redeemer Liveth

Greeting Brothers and Sisters! There is a man in the word of God who makes a statement that I believe is one of the most powerful quotes in the Bible. This man is experiencing extreme turmoil and trauma. He has an unsympathetic friend by the name of Bildad who calls him wicked, almost insinuating he is in the predicament he's in due to his own errors. He asks his so called friends, "how long will you vex my soul, and break me in pieces with your words?" He's so upset with all of these accusations that he looks at his friends and tells them, "I didn't do this to myself. If you want to know who has put me in this net, you're going to have to talk to God. For I am in this predicament because of him." By now I'm sure you know that I am referring to Job.

Many of us, if not all of us, have been upset or distraught about situations in our lives that we can neither understand nor explain. It seems like it is in those times when the Lord steps in to remind us that He is still with us. I believe with all my heart this is what happened to Job. After all of Job's complaining, Job comes to his senses and says these words (I'm paraphrasing), "Wait a minute everyone, I know you hear my anger, disappointment and frustration, but I want you to know how I really feel, FOR I KNOW MY REDEEMER LIVETH. And though after my skin worms destroy this body, yet in my flesh shall I see God." Job may have gotten distracted by his trials and tribulations and displayed his anger, but not to the point where he lost total confidence in God.

No matter what you are facing or going through, remember that we have a risen Savior waiting to intervene on our behalf. It is in our times of weakness He shows Himself strong, in our times of confusion, He makes our way plain, and in our times of despair that He brings great joy.

_____

_____

_____

_____

_____

_____

_____

_____

_____

_____

_____

_____

_____

_____

_____

_____

_____

_____

Lift Me Up Week 48

Good Tidings of Joy

Greetings Brothers and Sisters! If your reading is tracking with the calendar year, in a week or so, many of us will be commemorating and celebrating the birth of our Lord and Savior Jesus Christ. I must say as wonderful as this day is, it is disappointing that the world has commercialized this day with an outward manifestation and display of festive activities that have very little or nothing at all to do with Jesus. And please don't misunderstand what I am trying to say, for in a few days, I too will be in one of the largest discount department stores looking for gifts for three of my young, angelic grandchildren. ☺ However, I don't want to miss the purpose and meaning of this day. And I pray that all of us will take heed to the angel of the Lord in Luke 2:10-14 as he proclaims not just to the wise men but to all the people, "Fear not, for behold, I bring you good tidings of (not just joy) but of GREAT joy." And he ends the 14th verse by saying, "Glory to God in the highest, and on earth peace, good will toward men."

I pray that wherever you are during this holiday season you do not feel pressured to overspend just to put more boxes under the tree, or that a spirit of sadness or depression comes over you if you find yourself unable to buy everything your kids or loved ones desire. I truly pray that love, peace and joy abound in your hearts and that you will give praise and honor to the honoree, the actual reason for the season.

_____

_____

_____

_____

_____

_____

_____

_____

_____

_____

_____

_____

_____

_____

_____

_____

_____

_____

_____

_____

_____

_____

_____

Lift Me Up Week 49

A Quiet And Peaceful Life

Greeting Brothers and Sisters! I read about several powerful things in one verse this week that I believe most people desire in their life today. Before I disclose what these powerful things are, I would first like to tell you a couple of things they aren't; money and success. The reason I make this point is because society tells you money and success will make you happy. And while they may bring happiness or some form of satisfaction, money and success do not symbolize some ultimate arrival at a supreme destination in life. Timothy says in First Timothy 2:1, "Supplications, prayers, intercessions, and giving of thanks must be made for all men." He is not referring only to the male gender when he says all men, but rather all humanity. He also tells us to pray for kings and all that are in authority. He states if supplications (speaking to God earnestly and humbly), prayers (communing and listening, petitioning or adoration to God), intercessions (praying to God on behalf of others) and giving thanks are present, you can have these powerful things in your life.

Okay, if you're unfamiliar with this passage of scripture I'm sure the suspense is getting to you. What are these powerful things, you ask? They are simple: peace, quiet, godliness and honesty. First Timothy states if you do all the things listed above, you can lead or (live) a quiet and peaceful life.

Many times when we think of quiet and peaceful we think of silence. I'm sure we can all recall times in our lives when the Lord gave us peace in the midst of our storm. The next thing he says is you can live this life in all godliness. Titus 2:12 gives us our best example of living a life of godliness and that is "living righteously, and godly, in this present world." And finally he says "live this life honestly," which means to live truthful, honorable and fair.

I think it is interesting that Timothy makes it very clear that the only way to live this quiet and peaceful life is through a diversity of prayer. Prayer is a powerful tool. It allows you to intercede on behalf of family and friends, spend time getting closer to God and it brings peace, quiet, godliness and honesty into your life. If you desire to experience these powerful things in your life, this week make it a point to carve out time for supplication, prayer, intercession and giving thanks to God for all things. When you do this, watch your environment and circumstances begin to transform.

Lift Me Up Week 50

How Bright Is Your Light?

Greetings Brothers and Sisters! The world is looking for you. The question is, will they find you? There is no better time than now for us to be witnesses for the Lord. Matthew 5:16 tells us to, "Let your light so shine before men, that they may see your good works, and glorify your Father which is in heaven." You don't have to be a great orator, skillful showman or as saintly as Mother Theresa to let your light shine. People simply need to see the Lord in you.

Acts chapter three highlights the story of an individual with a disability seeking assistance. This gentleman was lame and was brought to the temple gate called "Beautiful" daily begging for money or food. When he saw Peter and John go into the temple he asked for alms. They first stopped to have a conversation with him. Then Peter does something that most people won't do because they don't want to be bothered. He fastens his eyes on him. He actually made eye to eye contact with this man in need. It is evident to me that Peter understood the power that resided in him as a Christian, the next three words that Peter speaks are the most powerful words a Christian can say about themselves, he says, "Look on us." You may not have to literally say these words about yourself, but as a Christian, someone should be looking at you and desiring the Christ that resides in you.

We live in an age where people put their entire life on display via Facebook, Twitter, Snapchat, reality television and more. They post their food, their outfits, their travel plans, they even post their pets. With all these new platforms, we Christians should take full advantage of the opportunity to show the love of Christ and win as many souls for the kingdom as possible. The world is watching you, let's give them a Holy Ghost, power filled, Christ-like show!

_____

_____

_____

_____

_____

_____

_____

_____

_____

_____

_____

_____

_____

_____

_____

_____

_____

Lift Me Up Week 51

One Lost Sheep

Greeting Brothers and Sisters! The story of the one lost sheep found in Luke 15:1-7 is one of the most fascinating parables in the Bible. Most preachers who speak on this parable focuses on the one lost sheep, but I want to share in this session a little insight of what the Lord has given me about the ninety-nine. We understand the message of the one lost sheep that wanders off from the fold, and the love Jesus displays to retrieve it. He is telling this story to the murmuring Pharisees and scribes who have a problem with Jesus receiving and eating with sinners. He addresses them with this question, "What man of you, having an hundred sheep, if he loses one of them, doth not leave the ninety and nine and go after the one that is lost, and rejoices over the one he has found." This is a wonderful example of the Lord not only saving you but making sure you stay saved.

This is my personal perception in reference to the ninety-nine. He doesn't just leave the ninety-nine in an open field or a safe place, but he leaves them in the wilderness. A wild and uncultivated region, uninhabited. One definition says this about the wilderness, it is ONLY inhabited by wild animals. Another definition says a wilderness is a confusing multitude or mass. I believe the fact that Jesus leaves the ninety-nine in the wilderness gives credence to his deity. I believe the Lord was demonstrating that He is able to watch and protect the ninety-nine in the wilderness and also go after this one lost sheep. Which confirms to me that He is omnipresent.

It is interesting to me that the one man in John 20:27-28 who doubted that Jesus was raised from the dead is the man that understood who Jesus really was. Jesus said to Thomas, "Reach thy finger, and behold my hands, and reach hither thy hand, and thrust it into my side." When Thomas realizes it was Jesus he said unto him, "MY LORD AND MY GOD," (Now I'm getting ready to preach). Before Thomas touched Jesus, Jesus said this to him, "Be not faithless, but believe." Jesus knew that Thomas was a doubter, but he was giving him another opportunity to believe.

In your trying times you may think that Jesus is only looking for that one lost sheep that have strayed away from the fold and has forgotten about those of you who have been faithful in your devotion, faithful to church, faithful in giving and walking upright before the Lord. But I want to reassure you that nowhere in this parable do you read that one of the ninety-nine were ever harmed in spite of their wilderness experience. Jesus gives great attention to bringing our lost brothers and sisters home, but He gives just as much attention with loving and caring for those of you who have remained faithful to the fold. Be encouraged, you're not forgotten.

Lift Me Up Week 52

A Thank You to My Readers

Thank you for going on this journey with me. I am thrilled I was able to share my words with readers from across the globe. I pray you were able to find connectivity and relevance in the topics. But I pray most of all you were truly lifted up. Please consider blessing a friend, family member, colleague or any acquaintance with a copy of Lift Me Up. Perhaps they will also be encouraged, motivated and lifted up.

Thank you again for giving me the opportunity to share my heart with you through this book. God bless you.

Loretta Earl-Miller